Accountability-Based Reforms

Donald F. Moores, General Editor

Volume 1   *Accountability-Based Reforms: The Impact on Deaf and Hard*
of Hearing Students
Stephanie W. Cawthon

Accountability-Based Reforms

The Impact on Deaf and Hard of Hearing Students

Stephanie W. Cawthon

Gallaudet University Press   WASHINGTON, D.C.

The Deaf Education Series
A Series Edited by Donald F. Moores

Gallaudet University Press
Washington, DC 20002

http://gupress.gallaudet.edu
© 2011 by Gallaudet University
All rights reserved. Published 2011
Printed in the United States of America

Library of Congress Cataloging-in-Publication Data

Cawthon, Stephanie W.
Accountability-based reforms : the impact on deaf and hard of hearing students / Stephanie W.
  Cawthon.
     p. cm.
  Includes bibliographical references and index.
  ISBN-13: 978-1-56368-485-2 (casebound : alk. paper)
  ISBN-10: 1-56368-485-3 (casebound : alk. paper)
    1. Deaf—Education—United States.   2. Educational accountability—United States.
3. Educational change—United States.   I. Title.
  HV2537.C39 2011
  371.91′2—dc22   2011000866

♾ The paper used in this publication meets the minimum requirements of
American National Standard for Information Sciences—Permanence of Paper for
Printed Library Materials, ANSI Z39.48–1984.

To My Parents

Contents

Preface

The initial impetus for this book began during my graduate studies in Educational Psychology at the University of Wisconsin-Madison. My personal and professional background is grounded in language and literacy development for students who are deaf or hard of hearing. Yet, until my doctoral studies, this work was largely de-contextualized from the educational systems that served this student population. While in graduate school and in the years that followed, I had the opportunity to work with teachers and district administrators who were grappling with how to implement large-scale educational reforms with students with such diverse linguistic and academic backgrounds. The reality of educating students who are deaf or hard of hearing within a systemic framework, with factors that carried both from the student level and from the larger state and federal level, challenged me to look at the impact of educational policies on deaf education from both an interdisciplinary and interactional lens.

Accountability-based educational reforms of the early years of this century seek to improve academic outcomes for *all* students. The most significant educational accountability reform in the United States, the No Child Left Behind Act of 2001 (NCLB), specifically stated that its purpose was to "close the achievement gap" between different student groups. The emphasis on the entire student body was an important shift because it represented a move toward a more inclusive definition of what (and who) "counts" in measures of school success. For years, school reform efforts either targeted students in regular education or those with special needs, but not both. The challenge of the current reforms is to establish policies that integrate the needs of students previously served under separate frameworks.

The purpose of this book is to look specifically at how elements of accountability-based education reform affect students who are deaf or hard of hearing. Very little of the information available about the impact of accountability reform identifies the effects on specific subgroups of students with disabilities. A general educational reform designed for all students may fall short when applied to students from diverse backgrounds; there may also be new opportunities for growth and visibility on the larger agendas that guide educational initiatives. Students who are deaf or hard of hearing participate in unique educational, linguistic, and cultural contexts that may interact with accountability efforts in both intended and unintended ways. In the past, many students who are deaf or hard of hearing have faced significant obstacles to reaching grade-level proficiency goals that are the hallmark of accountability reforms. There is a need, therefore, for a specific exposition of how accountability reform affects deaf education. Using the NCLB structure as a starting point, this book presents and discusses key assumptions behind accountability reforms and how they affect students who are deaf or hard of hearing, their teachers, and their families. This inquiry, in turn, can lead to important questions about what it means to conceptualize an accountability-based education reform for *all* students.

Federally directed legislation provides a starting point for conversations about the efficacy of an accountability approach to raising student achievement. This volume will explore both where we have seen some of the implications of accountability-based education reform for students who are deaf or hard of hearing and areas where the design of a federal system leaves only questions about the implications for deaf education. The perspectives in this book reflect the unique federal-state relationship found in the United States, with shared governance of school systems and, across states, independent mechanisms for defining student success. The sequence of this book first gives the reader a brief introduction to the deaf education context (Chapter 1) and accountability-based education reforms (Chapter 2). Chapters 3 through 7 each address a central issue that arises from the intersection of accountability reform components and students who are deaf or hard of hearing. These chapters give an overview of an important component of accountability reform, available research, and how it has been implemented in the United States. Stemming from this foundation, each chapter includes recommendations for future action by educators, parents, researchers, and education policy makers. Chapter 8 closes the book with a synthesis of themes that cut across the narrative as a whole.

The primary audience for this book is individuals who directly experience accountability policies as they impact students who are deaf or hard of hearing. Teachers, administrators, and parents are thus the primary audience for this book. Psychologists, counselors, speech-language therapists, interpreters, and students in disability or deaf studies programs may also find this book useful in their preparation for working with students who are deaf or hard of hearing. The hope is to provide sufficient background and context on students who are deaf or hard of hearing and accountability mechanisms to lead to a meaningful reflection on the implications of externally driven reforms. Students in teacher preparation programs, especially those who are interested in issues that may apply to students with disabilities or English Language Learners, may also find this volume to be a helpful resource. Finally, there will also be some important policy considerations for individuals designing future large-scale accountability reforms. The design of an accountability-based reform requires both simplicity, so that it can be implemented most clearly, and flexibility, so that it can be applied to a range of educational and social contexts. The case of deafness and education for students who are deaf or hard of hearing is a useful example of how a national education initiative can impact specific sub-populations in different, often unintended, ways. Findings from this book may therefore be applicable to policy development that considers low-incidence disability groups and students from diverse backgrounds.

My overall intent in this book is to provide a bridge between the unique educational context of students who are deaf or hard of hearing and analysis of the broad accountability policies that are applied to all students in public education. The challenge in a federal education reform is to provide guidelines that enhance, and do not detract from, the learning outcomes for students. By articulating these connections and laying out areas for future consideration, this book hopes to provide a context for evaluating the potential effectiveness of educational accountability reforms. Many of the examples here are from NCLB, but the focus is on the larger scope of accountability as a way of improving student outcomes and closing achievement gaps. I hope that this contribution can stimulate that discussion as we strategize how we as an educational community can address issues raised by accountability reform. I encourage the reader to reflect on where these implications are significant in their own contexts and to continue the dialogue as we continue onward towards goal of academic success for all students.

Accountability-Based Reforms

1

The Deaf Education Context

The purpose of this chapter is to describe the context of deaf education in an effort to better understand how accountability reforms may affect students who are deaf or hard of hearing. One debated assumption about public primary and secondary education is that, as a whole, it is in great need of repair. Does this same assumption apply to the educational structures that serve students who are deaf or hard of hearing (Johnson, 2003b; Simms & Thumann, 2007; Steffan, 2004)? This chapter first discusses demographics of today's population of students who are deaf or hard of hearing—a diverse group with great variability in language use, educational experiences, and academic success. The chapter then briefly discusses educational placement and its relationship with how we evaluate potential effectiveness of accountability reforms. Students who are deaf or hard of hearing attend a variety of settings, for example, some attend schools for the deaf with specifically tailored instruction and cohorts of students who are deaf or hard of hearing, and some attend schools with very little Deaf-centered[1] pedagogy or student resources.

---

1. Designations of "Deaf" or "deaf" vary across individuals, groups, and contexts. In this volume, *Deaf* refers to contexts where the emphasis is on a cultural community or identify construct. Deaf communities and identities tend to include a signed language as primary means of communication (e.g., American Sign Language). If the original author refers to *Deaf* in his or her

Academic success depends largely on a student's ability to read; literacy development is a main area of concentration in the research literature on the effectiveness of instruction for students who are deaf or hard of hearing. This chapter therefore discusses several strands of research related to literacy development in deaf education. The chapter concludes with recommendations for how an understanding of the demographics of students who are deaf or hard of hearing the field might lead to advocacy efforts for this student population within accountability-based education reform.

Student Demographics

This first section discusses what we know about the prevalence of students who are deaf or hard of hearing in the United States as well as key characteristics of this diverse population. Three relevant themes to this discussion are that (a) students who are deaf or hard of hearing make up a low-incidence population; (b) many students who are deaf or hard of hearing have other disabilities; and (c) the growing use of cochlear implants may change the future linguistic and communication patterns among students who are deaf or hard of hearing.

For the purpose of this discussion of accountability reforms in public education, it is important to know how many students in the elementary and secondary grades (i.e., Kindergarten to Grade 12) have a hearing loss (Mitchell & Karchmer, 2005, 2006). The U.S. Department of Education estimates that a total of just over 72,000 deaf or hard of hearing students receive services under the Individuals With Disabilities Education Act (IDEA) nationwide (U.S. Office of Special Education Programs, 2004). This total does not count those deaf or hard of hearing students who are not eligible for IDEA. This number also does not include children for whom another disability is considered the *primary* disability. For example, if a child has both a learning disability and a hearing loss, but the learning disability is considered the primary disability, then that student would not be included in these totals for deaf or

---

discussion, I also adopt that descriptor. On the whole, the book uses "little-*d*" *deaf* because this form is the terminology used in education and policy circles. Furthermore, the collective term *deaf or hard of hearing* is used throughout the book to refer to individuals with a variety of characteristics, including different levels of hearing loss, use of amplification systems, and a range of communication systems.

hard of hearing students. Finally, these figures do not include many students who experience temporary hearing loss due to otitis media or other affecting conditions (Easterbrooks, 1999). The number of children in the United States who actually have a hearing loss will therefore be higher than the number who officially receive services in schools under IDEA. However, even if there are more than 72,000 students, the key point is that this group is still a very low-incidence population in the public schools (Blackorby & Knokey, 2006; Bowen & Ferrell, 2003; Mitchell, 2005). Through IDEA, U.S. public schools serve approximately 6 million students with disabilities; the estimated 72,000 students who are deaf or hard of hearing represent roughly 1% of the students with disabilities population.

Many students whose primary disability is categorized as deaf or hard of hearing also have other disabilities (Gallaudet Research Institute, 2008). Approximately 40% of students counted in the 2007–08 Gallaudet Annual Survey were listed as having an additional disability. In a national profile of students in the Special Education Elementary Longitudinal Study (also known as SEELS), about half of parents of students with hearing loss indicated that their child had an additional disability (Blackorby & Knokey, 2006). Additional disabilities include learning disabilities, speech impairment, cerebral palsy, mental retardation, emotional disturbance, and attention deficit disorder. As with the general population, the incidence of autism and autistic spectrum disorder is rising quickly among deaf and hard of hearing students (Vernon & Rhodes, 2009). A student who is deaf or hard of hearing with multiple disabilities will often face great challenges in attaining grade-level academic proficiency. Yet discussions of the implications of education reform on students with disabilities as a whole, including students who are deaf or hard of hearing, often do not take into account the significant challenges faced by students with multiple disabilities (Cawthon, 2007; see Guardino, 2008, for a summary and implications and Bruce, DiNatale, & Ford, 2008, for a discussion of needed professional development).

Before initiatives to identify children with hearing loss at an early age, diagnosis of students who are deaf or hard of hearing often came late into their language development years. As a result, many children had decreased exposure to language (either speech or sign language) during what is considered a sensitive period for language and cognitive development. The Universal Newborn Hearing Screening program, authorized by the Public Health

Service Act, Title III, Section 301, 42 U.S.C. 241, provides federal funds for states to screen infants for hearing loss before they leave the hospital (for a discussion of similar initiatives in other countries, see Storbeck & Calvert-Evans, 2008). In states with screening programs, children with potential hearing loss receive follow-up information and connections with resources within the community at the very earliest stages of language development.

Early identification of hearing loss has led to a greater emphasis on amplification and oral communication options for students who are deaf or hard of hearing (Vohr, 2003; Yoshinaga-Itano & Gravel, 2001). In the past few years, a growing number of children with the most significant hearing losses have undergone cochlear implant surgery (Belzner & Seal, 2009; Niparko & Blankenhorn, 2003). In a person with functioning hearing, the inner ear acts to convert sounds into electric impulses that are then sent to the brain (U.S. Food and Drug Administration, 2004). Although the cochlear implant does not create normal hearing, it can give auditory input to the brain to help process speech and other sounds (Barker & Tomblin, 2004). According to the Gallaudet Research Institute 2007–08 Annual Survey, approximately 14% of children attending schools or programs for deaf or hard of hearing students had a cochlear implant (Gallaudet Research Institute, 2008). Cochlear implants have been on the rise steadily over the last decade: cochlear implant use among children has grown by approximately 1% per year between 1999 and 2007. Although implantation trends may shift in the future, use of cochlear implants among students who are deaf or hard of hearing is currently experiencing a steady increase.

Cochlear implants have potentially far-reaching implications for the Deaf community (Christiansen & Leigh, 2002; Marschark & Spencer, 2006; Moores, 2006; Simms & Thumann, 2007). Proponents of cochlear implants view the procedure as medically safe and an effective means of giving deaf children access to the sounds of speech (Geers, 2002). Research has provided some evidence for increased speech and language outcomes when implantation is followed by consistent, intensive speech therapy (Blamey, Sarant, Paatsch, Barry, Bow, Wales et al., 2001; Geers & Brenner, 2004; Moog, 2002; Tomblin, Spencer, Flock, Tyler, & Gantz, 1999). Yet those who object to cochlear implants note the severity of brain surgery on those very young children within the population who cannot give informed consent (Lane, 1999;

Moores, 2006). Not all children who have an implant follow predicted trajectories of speech and language development (Duchesne, Sutton, & Bergeron, 2009) and often need to use sign language for effective communication (Moores, 2009; Nussbaum, La Porta, & Hinger, 2003). Furthermore, the level of speech therapy required is potentially intrusive and expensive given the possibly limited gain.

The above three demographic characteristics of students who are deaf or hard of hearing have implications for how we investigate the impact of accountability reforms on this population. First, low-incidence populations are often aggregated into summaries of student outcomes across multiple groups, so outcomes for those with characteristics or educational needs very different from those of students who are deaf or hard of hearing are often combined. Nevertheless, being a part of the larger "students with disabilities" umbrella may be beneficial when gaining access to resources such as those through the Americans With Disabilities Act of 1990. However, aggregation of low-incidence populations can also mask some of the unique characteristics of each subgroup, resulting in muddied waters for not only addressing educational needs but also implementing educational reform. As we will discuss further in Chapter 4, it is very difficult to determine the status of students who are deaf or hard of hearing under the current accountability system.

The second demographic characteristic is the presence of multiple disabilities. Additional disabilities add to the complexity of language, communication, and instruction for students with hearing loss. For example, a Deaf student who also has a learning disability may require additional support beyond a sign language interpreter to experience academic success. Most summaries of students who are deaf or hard of hearing rely on information from students who have a *primary* designation for hearing loss. Yet up to half of these students are likely to have a second disability. Summaries of academic performance based only on the primary disability reduce our understanding of how students who are deaf or hard of hearing fare under educational reform. Inversely, some students with hearing loss have other primary disabilities and, thus, may not be recognized as a member of the deaf or hard of hearing subgroup. Most performance summaries of students who are deaf or hard of hearing do not include students with hearing loss as a secondary disability. The goal of accountability reform is to make measures of student achievement more transparent. For students who are deaf or hard of hearing, it is necessary to include both groups—students with primary *and* secondary hearing loss designations—to meet that goal.

Third, the use of cochlear implants with children, discussed above, brings with it some evidence for improved speech and language in particular circumstances, but it also brings its own set of controversies and concerns. Evidence of improvements must be further verified, and concerns, not only for safety and health reasons but also for financial reasons, need to be addressed.

In summary, heterogeneity in the deaf and hard of hearing population has always been a challenge for the field. When making recommendations about changes for instructional strategies in deaf education or best practices in teacher preparation, the characteristics of students in the research base is critical to making predictions about the effectiveness of changes for this diverse group (Antia, Jones, Reed, & Kreimeyer, 2009; Johnson, Liddell, & Erting, 1989). Educational policy that supports a "one size fits all" approach to instruction and assessment risks misapplying strategies designed with "typical" students in mind. This risk of misapplication is particularly true for students who are deaf or hard of hearing. In Chapters 4 and 5, we will investigate ways that assessment and accountability approaches oversimplify the learning process for students who are deaf or hard of hearing with multiple disabilities.

Finally, accountability reform (as are all large-scale reforms) is applied on top of, and not instead of, the local educational context. In deaf education, cochlear implants and the controversy surrounding their use is part of the local context of how parents, teachers, and students approach education. The use of a medical procedure to change the impact of a disability may not apply only to children who are deaf. Its potential interpretation as an agenda for eradicating a culture and way of life is, however, unique to the Deaf community. One argument in favor of cochlear implants is that implants may help children who have profound hearing loss be more fully mainstreamed into regular education classrooms by improving speech and subsequent academic achievement. When accountability reforms measure the effectiveness of schools from a single perspective, with English as the primary mechanism for demonstrating language and academic proficiency, it is possible that the reforms become a way to gather evidence for or against cochlear implantation. In a sense, this strategy may be a case of using the end goal of English proficiency to promote the success of cochlear implants. This unintended consequence of accountability reform may have significant impact on how it is implemented in the Deaf community.

Educational Setting

Student demographics are but one area where there is diversity within deaf education. Educational setting is also more varied for students who are deaf or hard of hearing than for students in regular education (Marschark, Lang, & Albertini, 2002). The history behind education for deaf students includes initiatives at the federal level. The Education of the Deaf Act, most recently amended in 2008, provides funding for the education of deaf students in elementary, secondary, and postsecondary settings. Gallaudet University (originally Gallaudet College, founded in 1864) and the National Institute of the Deaf at Rochester Institute of Technology are both funded through this legislation. As part of its charge, Gallaudet also hosts the Kendall Demonstration School and the Model Secondary School for the Deaf. Collectively, these federally funded institutions serve as centers of educational research, resources for teacher preparation, and advocacy for parents and teachers across the country.

Depending on the setting, a student who is deaf or hard of hearing may be enrolled either with deaf or hard of hearing peers in a regional program that combines separate and integrated instruction or as a single student integrated into a regular education classroom (Blackorby & Knokey, 2006). These are common, but not mutually exclusive, designations. For example, some schools for the deaf may offer instructional support services in district programs or regular educational settings. The overlap in categories can make an educational setting difficult to characterize from site to site. Another useful designation is the percentage of time students who are deaf or hard of hearing spend with hearing peers. In the 2007–08 Gallaudet Annual Survey, with a sample skewed largely toward students at schools for the deaf, only a quarter of students spent more than 25 hours per week with hearing peers. Half spent no more than 5 hours per week in an integrated format. By looking at both time spent with hearing peers and the location designation, researchers and policymakers can gain a better understanding of the characteristics of each educational setting for students who are deaf or hard of hearing (Mitchell & Karchmer, 2006).

Along with the diverse settings is variability in the roles of educational professionals who work with students who are deaf or hard of hearing. For example, students may be served by a teacher of the deaf, a special educator, or by a regular education teacher with an educational interpreter. Teachers of the deaf are professionals who have been trained in professional programs that focus on deaf education. A special education teacher, in contrast, receives preparation that applies to the broad spectrum of students with disabilities. It is possible that a special education teacher will not have specific training in the language and communication strategies to use with students who are deaf or hard of hearing. Regular education teachers are the most common type of educator of students who are deaf or hard of hearing (Muller, 2005a). Their professional preparation includes little to no formal training in pedagogy for students with disabilities, students who are English Language Learners, or students who are deaf or hard of hearing. When a regular education teacher has students who use sign language, an educational interpreter translates the teacher's spoken language for the student. Each kind of teacher training lends to a particular emphasis and skill set used by teachers of students who are deaf or hard of hearing. Educational settings employ teachers with different preparation and certification and, thus, draw on different strengths and resources. As we will discuss in Chapter 6, teachers in different professional roles experience teacher-quality components of accountability reform in different ways.

Educational placement for students who are deaf or hard of hearing has changed significantly in the last 30 years. Much of this change is due to larger inclusion movements and implementation of IDEA (Stinson & Antia, 1999). IDEA stipulates that students must be taught in the "least restrictive environment" (LRE) possible. Depending on how LRE and the needs of the student are interpreted, IDEA can result in a push toward regular education settings and away from separate settings such as schools for the deaf. Figure 1.1 shows the results of demographic surveys conducted through the Gallaudet Research Institute (GRI) in each of the last three decades (Gallaudet Research Institute, 2008; Karchmer, Allen, & Brown, 1988). These surveys divide student placement into three categories: (a) schools for the deaf, (b) programs for deaf students in general education settings, and (c) regular education classrooms. As time has passed, the Annual Survey has become more representative of schools for the deaf than other settings; the overall population of

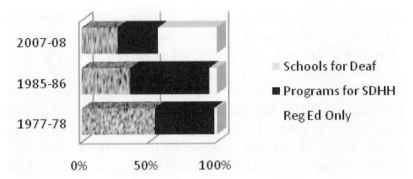

Figure 1.1. Educational placement trends for deaf and hard of hearing students. Data from *Deaf Students and Their Schools: The Changing Demographics* by T. Karchmer, M. Allen, & S. Brown, 1988, Washington, DC: Gallaudet Research Institute, and *Regional and National Summary Report of Data From the 2007–08 Annual Survey of Deaf and Hard of Hearing Children and Youth* by Gallaudet Research Institute, 2008, Washington, DC: Author.

students who are deaf or hard of hearing has a greater proportion of students in regular education settings than is reported below (Mitchell, 2004).

In interpreting this graph, it is helpful to look at the relative proportion of students at each site within each year. The proportion of students who are deaf or hard of hearing in schools exclusively serving deaf students has declined whereas the proportion in regular education has increased significantly during this time frame. This transition happened in phases over the three decades. The most dramatic shift between 1977 and 1985 was the proportion of students moving from schools for the deaf to programs for students who are deaf or hard of hearing in regular education settings (trend confirmed in Holden-Pitt & Diaz, 1998). This shift reflects the move toward integration with hearing peers (Bello, 2007; Blackorby & Knokey, 2006). Yet even more striking is the significant jump in regular education placements in the 1990s and 2000s (Moores, 2004). Regular education placements more than tripled in the last decade. This shift is partly a result of reduction in the number of stand-alone schools or merging of program resources (Asmar, 2006; Blackorby & Knokey, 2006; Silverman, 2006). However, in spite of these long-term shifts, placement trends have stabilized over the last few years, particularly for students with severe or profound hearing losses (Blackorby & Knokey, 2006; Gallaudet Research Institute, 2001, 2005, 2008). Children of Deaf adults, those with significant hearing losses, and those with multiple disabilities are more likely to enroll in schools for the deaf than students with more moderate losses or those who have hearing parents. Schools for the deaf may serve fewer students than in the past overall, but they still play a critical role in the education of students who are deaf or hard of hearing.

One area not evident in the overall graphs is the change in the age range of students served in the different educational settings. In the past, students at schools for the deaf would attend from their early elementary through high school years. More recent trends are for students to remain in a local elementary school at a regional program or in a regular education school for the elementary years. Students who are deaf or hard of hearing, particularly those who are Deaf, then shift to a school for the deaf in the secondary grades (Cawthon & the Online Research Lab, 2006; personal communication, Diana Poeppelmeyer, May 14, 2009). At schools for the deaf, this shift places a greater emphasis on the educational needs of secondary students. In the context of academic outcomes for accountability reform, the focus at schools for the deaf may therefore shift to academic content in upper grades and on high school completion (Lang, 2002).

Educational setting has implications for accountability in two ways: measurement and transparency. First, accountability explicitly measures student outcomes in public education. Depending on how the reform is structured, this measurement could focus on individual students, teachers, schools, districts, or states. The organizational unit (e.g., school or program) responsible for educating students therefore is relevant to the concept of measuring and "holding accountable" the education system for student achievement. In current accountability reforms, *schools* are the most local organizational unit evaluated for student progress. One challenge in the shifts in school enrollment for students who are deaf or hard of hearing is that it is difficult for schools to reliably measure how their students fare over time. This difficulty is particularly true if the demographic makeup of the study body changes (e.g., influx of secondary students at schools for the deaf) from year to year. Thus, accountability reform can be a tool for schools or programs to use in their own self-assessment, but it must take into consideration the fact that different student cohorts arrive each year. Chapter 5 will discuss in further detail how schools for the deaf, district programs for students who are deaf or hard of hearing, and regular education programs are differentially affected by the current structure of accountability reforms.

On the flip side of this discussion of educational setting and accountability reform is the level of transparency provided in the structure of the law. If the "unit of responsibility" is broad enough that student performance is calculated over a large group, we lose information about how smaller groups are served by that institution. It is easy to lose specific information about how low-incidence groups fare in large-scale reforms, and students who are deaf or hard of hearing in accountability reforms are no exception. The majority of students who are deaf or hard of hearing are in regular education programs that have only a handful of students with hearing loss in the school or district. In some cases, the deaf or hard of hearing "group" for a school is a single student. When report cards are given to schools, especially regular education schools that may serve only one or a few students who are deaf or hard of hearing, the group progress of students who are deaf or hard of hearing cannot be tracked. In other words, if a student who is deaf or hard of hearing is in a regular education school, it is unlikely that we would ever know how well that student performed on state assessments. A state could aggregate results for all individual students who are deaf or hard of hearing across the state, a recommendation I strongly support, but it is challenging to report this information from a single school or district without violating federal privacy laws and confidentiality of student information. The current focus on overall population summaries (e.g., all students with disabilities) thus limits what we know about the impact of changes made at the local level (e.g., instruction to students who are deaf or hard of hearing at a local program).

Academic Outcomes for Students Who Are Deaf or Hard of Hearing

Accountability reform focuses almost exclusively on student performance on standardized assessments as a measure of successful education (Chapter 4 discusses testing issues in greater detail). One of the underlying challenges in deaf education is the history of poor performance on large-scale standardized tests. Test performance on these tests is, on average, lower for deaf students than for hearing students, although performance relative to hearing peers varies by domain (Brasel & Quigley, 1977; Harris & Bamford, 2001; Mutua & Elhoweris, 2002; Ronnberg, 2003; Traxler, 2000). For example, on one older standardized assessment study, deaf adolescents performed at a fourth-grade level on reading comprehension but at a seventh-grade level on mathematics (Holt, Traxler, & Allen, 1992). Discrepancies between hearing and deaf student groups were also larger for reading comprehension than for mathematics: deaf students' mean reading scores varied from two to six grades below the mean for hearing students, with the gap increasing with advancing grade. The mathematics component fared better: the mean for young deaf students was only one grade below grade level and stayed within three grades levels throughout the cross-sectional sample. While there is a great deal of variability in student achievement in math and reading (e.g., Ansell & Pagliaro, 2006; Antia et al. 2009), these average trends have remained relatively stable into recent years (Qi & Mitchell, 2007).

The focus of accountability reform is on reducing the achievement gap between student groups. Although teachers indicate that state assessments can provide useful information about student progress at the local level (Luckner & Bowen, 2006), there is very little data available on the proficiency rates of students who are deaf or hard of hearing on state standardized assessments used for accountability (see Antia et al., 2009, for data on subsamples from Arizona and Colorado). There are two summaries available that look at student scores across individual schools or states: (a) studies by Cawthon and colleagues and (b) by the National Center on Low-Incidence Disabilities (2006). I have looked at the No Child Left Behind (NCLB) report cards for schools for the deaf for three years (Cawthon, 2004, 2007, 2008). On the whole, the achievement levels for students who are deaf or hard of hearing were no lower than for other groups of students with disabilities. In terms of proficiency on state standardized assessments, students who are deaf or hard of hearing scored mostly in the lower quartile (25% of students at the school being proficient at grade level). Perhaps surprisingly, there was *not* a consistent trend of higher scores in math than in reading. Yet there were several examples of high percentages of deaf and hard of hearing students meeting proficiency guidelines in the 2005–06 school year, particularly in Kansas, Maryland, South Carolina, and Texas. Several of these states had demonstrated similar levels of student achievement in previous years, strengthening the stability of this finding (Cawthon, 2004).

The National Center on Low-Incidence Disabilities (NCLID) has gathered available information from state departments of education for several low-incidence disability groups, including students who are deaf or hard of hearing (NCLID, 2007).). These summaries are for all public education students in the state, not just those who attend the publicly funded school for the deaf. The research is challenging because accountability reform does not require states to disaggregate their student achievement data by disability type. Those states that do are also sometimes reluctant to share this information with others (NCLID, 2007). Results combined scores across two to four states, depending on the grade and test subject. These averages therefore represent the percentage of students who meet state proficiency standards, but the way those standards are defined certainly varies for students in that group.

The Grade 4 and Grade 8 NCLID results for three groups—students who are deaf or hard of hearing, all students with disabilities, and students without disabilities—are shown in Table 1.1. For 2006 assessments, proficiency rates ranged from a low of 14.7% (Grade 4 English Language Arts, based on 185 students) to a high of 38.9% (Grade 4 Reading, based on 249 students). On the whole, science proficiency rates were lower than those for the other core academic areas (science was not assessed in every grade). This range of proficiency rates is a relatively small spread of scores considering assessments were for several grades (Grades 2–8) and subjects (ELA, Reading, Math, and Science). This spread is smaller than what was found when looking only at test scores for students at schools for the deaf, indicating that state disaggregations of scores may be more reliable estimates of student proficiency.

It is in this context that accountability reforms, with an emphasis on student performance on state achievement tests, come into play. The stakes are high; schools where few students meet annual benchmarks will face consequences and restrictions in how they spend their federal funds. For any school serving a traditionally underperforming (and at times, underserved) population, it can be frustrating to be measured against the state's overall goals without consideration for how far students need to improve to reach them. This situation is further complicated for students who are deaf or hard of hearing by the unique educational needs they often have, ones more challenging to overcome than those of students without disabilities. Research in deaf education focuses a great deal on issues surrounding literacy development and cultural factors. The remainder of this chapter therefore explores some of the potential challenges that students who are deaf or hard of hearing face in attaining grade-level proficiency in reading, a gateway skill to overall academic achievement.

Table 1.1. Grade 4 and Grade 8 State Assessments, 2006

| | Subject | | | | | | | |
| | ELA | | Reading | | Math | | Science | |
Student Group	Number Assessed	Percentage Proficient	Number Assessed	Percentage Proficient	Number Assessed	Percentage Proficient	Number Assessed	Percentage Proficient
Grade 4								
Without Disabilities	113,369	53.0%	25,726	30.4%	163,901	55.5%	N/A	N/A
All Disabilities	20,733	19.9%	249	38.9%	46,574	16.9%	N/A	N/A
Deaf or Hard of Hearing	185	14.7%	88	53.2%	436	34.9%	N/A	N/A
Grade 8								
Without Disabilities	125,631	65.0%	NA	N/A	179,050	46.7%	116,183	45.5%
All Disabilities	21,318	25.0%	28,679	24.5%	50,095	13.5%	15,855	11.6%
Deaf or Hard of Hearing	177	27.1%	312	35.0%	491	22.6%	191	12.7%

Reading as the Crux of the Matter

Reading skills are a critical component of compulsory education for all students because they serve as an access point for learning in many other domains. Literacy development is certainly the largest area of research in deaf education (Luckner & Cooke, 2010; Luckner & Handley, 2008). One reason for the focus on literacy is the long-standing difficulty education programs have had in teaching students who are deaf or hard of hearing how to read (Schimmel, Edwards, & Prickett, 1999; Truax, Fan, & Whitesell, 2004). It is proposed that many students who are deaf or hard of hearing do not become proficient readers because of delayed exposure to a fluent first-language base (Loeterman, Paul, & Donahue, 2002; Trezek & Wang, 2006). Strategies to improve literacy outcomes stem from a range of theories on literacy acquisition, including questions about the necessity of a phonological code as a precursor to decoding text (Nielsen & Luetke-Stahlman, 2002; Paul, 1994; Wang, Trezek, Luckner, & Paul, 2008, with response from Allen et al., 2009, and rejoinder from Paul, Wang, Trezek, & Luckner, 2009). Related aspects of literacy development, including content literacy and strategies used with students who are English Language Learners, are also a part of the discussion of how to improve literacy outcomes for students who are deaf or hard of hearing. Taken together, these elements form a foundation for discussion of what needs to be considered for an overall accountability reform when it measures academic progress and constructs initiatives to close the achievement gap (for a discussion of whether reading challenges are about reading or other factors, see Marschark et al., 2009).

There has been considerable debate over the best approach to literacy instruction for students who are deaf or hard of hearing. This debate has traditionally included discussions of phonologically based approaches to reading versus emphasis on visual reading cues, contextual evidence, and whole language approaches (Paul, 1997; Wang et al., 2008). This contrast is sometimes classified as a tension between "bottom-up" and "top-down" theories of the reading process. The bottom-up theories tend to be based on decoding English sounds and using the phonics to build reading skills (e.g., Nielsen & Luetke-Stahlman, 2002; Trezek & Wang, 2006; Wilbur, 2000). For example, in a bottom-up approach, a student might learn how to connect the pronunciation of the letter *b* with the printed letter at the start of the word *bus*. In contrast, the top-down theories focus on holistic strategies such as using natural sources of print to foster emergent reading skills, developing a world-knowledge base through native language (usually American Sign Language), and recognizing whole words (e.g., Ewoldt, 1990; Goldin-Meadow & Mayberry, 2001; Kuntze, 1998). For example, in a top-down approach, students might begin with telling a story about their dog, then work from that story to connections about the dog in pictures and then in words. The top-down approach relies less on knowing the phonological components of written English and more on access to print through other means.

Although the discussion about the emphasis on phonology continues, many researchers and practitioners now include both bottom-up and top-down elements in their recommendations for literacy instruction for students who are deaf or hard of hearing (Evans, 2004; Maxwell, 1986; Moores & Miller, 2001; Schirmer, 2000). The discussion is particularly relevant for those students who are deaf or hard of hearing with severe to profound hearing loss who have limited access to spoken language (Paul, 1997). Depending on the individual student's linguistic repertoire, different strategies may prove to be effective in bringing him up to grade level in reading. For example, reading instruction for beginning readers may target word recognition and vocabulary development because it is essential for later comprehension and reading fluency (e.g., Barker, 2003; Loeterman et. al, 2002; Luckner & Muir, 2002). Early reading instruction may therefore focus on a bottom-up approach to gaining the building blocks for reading. Reading instruction for older students might focus more on tying ideas to daily experiences or understanding the motivation behind the author's intentions, reflecting a top-down approach. Best practice recommendations for combined approaches are still in the beginning stages. The heterogeneity within the population of students who are deaf or hard of hearing as well as variation in educational setting and instructional staff members make it difficult to generalize findings beyond single studies. Empirical findings on the effectiveness of specific reading instruction strategies with students who are deaf or hard of hearing, with sufficient sample sizes to draw causal connections, are only now emerging in the research literature.

It can be difficult for students who are deaf or hard of hearing without grade-level literacy skills to learn other content areas such as science, social studies, etc., placing them at risk for academic and social failure (Howell &

Luckner, 2003). Although literacy is often taught as a separate part of the academic curriculum, some programs are looking at ways to integrate literacy instruction into other academic domains. These strategies, known as content literacy skills, are strategies that good readers use to tailor their learning to the academic context. For example, the reading comprehension strategies and vocabulary one may use when studying a chronological time line in a history course are different from those used when preparing for a chemistry experiment. In a history course, teachers might emphasize either concurrent events or the linear sequence of events using the time line as a conceptual anchor. In chemistry, teachers might first address the structure and layout of a science textbook to help the student feel confident about her ability to navigate it for content (Howell & Luckner, 2003). Text elements such as the headings, diagrams, and captions as well as content features such as structuring a logical argument help the student approach the course with less trepidation. (Researchers also tapped into mental imagery techniques to help the student learn new content-specific vocabulary, as found in Schirmer, Bailey, & Lockman, 2004). Finally, the student is taught how to summarize important information in long stretches of text. Using this approach, secondary students might gain needed skills not only in general literacy but also in academic course work. This research demonstrates the importance of using multiple strategies to improve student learning as well as ways to leverage both content and literacy skill development. Students who are deaf or hard of hearing with content literacy skills will be better prepared to succeed on measures of student proficiency as accountability reforms move from core content areas of math and reading into applied content areas of science and social studies.

Literacy and academic characteristics of students who are deaf or hard of hearing depend not only on degree of hearing loss but also on language use and access to culturally relevant academic experiences (Simms & Thumann, 2007). When thinking about the diversity of students who are deaf or hard of hearing and educational models to serve their needs, it can be helpful to look at parallels with other students who do not have spoken English as a first language. Some students who are deaf or hard of hearing share similarities not only with other students with disabilities but also with English Language Learners. For example, students who use American Sign Language as their first language may learn English as a second language. Some experiences of students who are deaf or hard of hearing can be similar to those of hearing students who come from a non-English speaking background and come to school with little to no English. The sensory access to English is different (visual vs. auditory), but the existence of a primary language base and different culture from that of the majority of the student body can be a common ground. Some researchers propose literacy development strategies for deaf students that are similar to those used with English Language Learners (Spaulding, Carolino, & Amen, 2004). Although not designated as special education students, English Language Learners require extra assistance as they simultaneously learn a new language and participate in the curriculum (Cummins, 1984). Two instructional strategies in deaf education reflect aspects of an English Language Learner framework applied to students who are deaf or hard of hearing: culturally relevant literacy and bilingual education.

There are multiple cultural elements at play for students in public education who are deaf or hard of hearing, including the roles of Deaf culture, sign language, and minority culture within American society (Van Cleve & Crouch, 1989; for an extensive discussion of status of Deaf Studies from multiple frameworks, see recent work by Hauser, O'Hearn, McKee, Steider, & Thew, 2010; Holocomb, 2010; Marschark & Humphries, 2010; Myers & Fernandes, 2009; Paul & Moores, 2010). Depending on the language contexts of their family and social contexts, students may also be bi- or trilingual (Gerner de Garcia, 1995, 2004). Qualls-Mitchell (2002) emphasizes the need to look at culturally relevant literacy curriculum for students who are deaf or hard of hearing. Qualls-Mitchell's research explores ways to use culturally relevant topics to engage students in reading activities. One of her key points is the need to build a culturally relevant vocabulary. In this approach, showing words along with images throughout the process is a foundational part of reading instruction for emerging readers. For Deaf students whose heritage is from the majority culture in the local community, connections may need to be made between American Sign Language and the hearing world. For students who are both Deaf and from a minority background, which will vary depending on the local context, a culturally relevant curriculum requires focusing on concepts and meaning that are relevant to all three cultures (Deaf, minority culture, and majority culture). The goal is to create a stimulating classroom environment that reflects the interests and diversity of the students.

If successful literacy is grounded in a student's language use, then the complexities of multilingual realities are important to address in reading development. Culturally relevant literacy approaches for students who are deaf or hard of hearing draw on student experiences in ways that integrate their linguistic and cultural background into the literacy acquisition process. When a bi- or tricultural approach is in place, literacy instruction can build on the child's ability to describe one's own experience. Yet most literacy curricula are taught from the perspective of the dominant, English-speaking, hearing culture (Simms & Thumann, 2007). Furthermore, accountability reforms in the United States emphasize English literacy development from the earliest grades to the detriment of multilingual approaches that may require additional time before English literacy is at grade level. When assessment focuses only on English literacy development, and not on literacy development in a broader sense, students from diverse language backgrounds are labeled as "non-proficient" readers at a time when they are still developing their English language skills.

Bilingual[2] education, reemerging in earnest about 30 years ago, is seen by some as a potentially fruitful model to use in educating deaf and hard of hearing students in a way that honors both the dominant English culture and the Deaf culture (e.g., Cangiano, 1992; Cline, 1997; LaSasso & Metzger, 1998; Laurence, 1991; Moores, 2008b; Wilbur, 2000; Zaitseva, Pursglove, & Gregory, 1999; for critiques, see also Mayer & Akamatsu, 1999; Stuckless, 1991). For students who are deaf or hard of hearing, the bilingual model combines American Sign Language and English in instruction. This strategy is, in part, a response to the perceived limitations of an oral-only or total communication (English with supplementary signs) environment. American Sign Language may be a more suitable first language for many students with hearing loss because it is communicated through the eyes, hands, and face. There is also emerging evidence of the strengths of bilingualism, including its effects in the areas of executive function and cognitive flexibility (Bialystok, Craik, & Ryan, 2006; Kushalnagar, Hannay, & Hernandez, 2010). Although the increase in cochlear implants may reduce the sole use of American Sign Language in instruction, American Sign Language will still play a role in the lives of students who are deaf or hard of hearing. Many hope that students who receive instruction in *both* American Sign Language and English will

---

2. Although I will primarily be discussing the bilingual education movement, many classrooms couple bilingual with bicultural emphases (Bi-Bi classrooms). Issues of culture are certainly important in discussing language development in deaf and hard of hearing children. The literature base, however, pertains almost exclusively to bilingual issues.

achieve higher levels of reading proficiency, and thus academic success, than those using only one mode of communication and instruction (Power, Hyde, & Leigh, 2008). The goal of the bilingual-bicultural movement reflects a "desire of many Deaf parents and parents of deaf children to have their children educated in an environment that supports and values both hearing and deaf culture and language" (Saunders, 1997, p. 62).

The concern for educators, however, is not so much that deaf students learn to *speak* English, but that they learn how to *read and write*. As Musselman (2000) points out, "arguments favoring one communication mode over another frequently hinge on its purported ability to facilitate literacy. Notions of reading, therefore, are central to current conceptualizations of deafness and deaf education" (p. 9). One driving assumption in the bilingual education model is that, although American Sign Language and English are distinct in many ways, American Sign Language is a robust language that can provide top-down reading comprehension skills for reading English. Although the syntax and lexical entries of American Sign Language are not directly transferable to English text, making inferences and connecting world knowledge very well may be. Bilingual education thus tries to leverage the strengths of the cultural knowledge accessible through visual language to improve comprehension of concepts presented in print.

Highlighting parallels between students who are deaf or hard of hearing and those who are English Language Learners is again useful in the context of bilingual education. The first application is on a structural level: both English Language Learners and students who are deaf or hard of hearing have programs dedicated to instructional strategies that meet their linguistic and academic needs. Programs and approaches that focus on cultural relevance and bilingual-bicultural education have the potential to bring elements of Deaf culture into the dialogue about education, both inside and outside of schools for the deaf. The second parallel is within the stated goal of accountability policy. One of the main priorities of NCLB is to close the achievement gap for students with disabilities and for ethnic minorities. Students who are deaf or hard of hearing and English Language Learners have historically poor educational outcomes, at least on measures of student achievement used in United States accountability reforms (Cawthon, 2004, 2007). Furthermore, NCLB also articulates the need to develop quality, language-rich programs for students who are English Language Learners and to, where possible, develop the first languages of students to be used as a basis for later English language development. Applied to students who are deaf or hard of hearing with a language/literacy delay, NCLB could be seen as a way to advocate for access to comprehensive language environments, including those with American Sign Language (Siegel, 2002). Therefore, from a large-scale and from a local (classroom-based) perspective, parallels between these two fields are important in this discussion about the impact of accountability reform on students who are deaf or hard of hearing.

Conclusion and Recommendations

Although students who are deaf or hard of hearing make up only a very small proportion of the overall student body, their unique linguistic, educational, and cultural characteristics make them an important case to study when investigating the impact of large-scale reforms on heterogeneous, low-incidence populations. The demographics of students who are deaf or hard of hearing highlight challenges related to primary and secondary categorizations of disability as well as the difficulty in understanding how reforms affect students with multiple disabilities. One recommendation mentioned in this chapter was to advocate for a summary of accountability measures specifically for students who are deaf or hard of hearing. This summary may have to occur at the state or national level and may be limited to common factors across states such as high school completion (the pending Common Core Content Standards Initiative may eventually provide a more broad basis for comparison across states). When looking at the effects of accountability reforms for students who are deaf or hard of hearing and who have multiple disabilities, it is important to know whether hearing loss is noted as a primary or secondary disability. An important effort would be to try and designate information in terms of (a) only students who are deaf or hard of hearing, (b) only students who are deaf or hard of hearing as a primary disability, and (c) only students who are deaf or hard of hearing as a secondary disability. This framing of data will give a more accurate picture of how students who are deaf or hard of hearing fare on measures of academic success with consideration for the heterogeneity of the student population.

Part of the complexity of looking at the effectiveness of instructional strategies for students with hearing loss is the diversity in approaches to literacy development. From the perspective of accountability reform, education for students who are deaf or hard of hearing may need to be strengthened in particular areas to raise academic outcomes. Although the purpose of large-scale reforms is not necessarily to prescribe specific instructional strategies, reforms can use accountability measures to motivate schools to use certain programs. For example, NCLB includes language supporting "evidenced-based" teaching for students learning to read. One recommendation that arises from this discussion is for the field to create an "evidence-based" database of instructional strategies for students who are deaf or hard of hearing. This database could be similar to that of the What Works Clearinghouse, formed at the national level by the U.S. Department of Education, but would be established and reviewed by professionals with the deaf education and research community. This database would need to include details such as (a) primary or secondary disability categories, (b) age range or literacy skill targeted with the instructional strategy, and (c) a description of the generalizability of findings to other students who are deaf or hard of hearing. An emerging research base related to literacy programs for students who are deaf or hard of hearing may support the details of accountability reform.

There are, however, additional strands of literacy development research that are relevant to the discussion of how to improve educational outcomes for students who are deaf or hard of hearing. Targeted learning strategies such as content literacy or test-taking skills are also important components of raising student proficiency on measures of achievement used in accountability frameworks. Culturally relevant or bilingual literacy approaches could be encouraged in a more flexible model of accountability that measures outcomes in these areas. One recommendation for advocates of students who are deaf or hard of hearing is to align, where possible, with advocates for students who are English Language Learners (August & Hakuta, 1997). For example, immigrant English Language Learners are exempt from English testing for the first three years that they are in the United States; a similar approach for students who are deaf or hard of hearing may allow for the needed time to develop English language skills before participating in English-based assessments. Accountability reform purports to raise achievement for all students; whether it can fulfill this promise depends on the ability of reforms to be responsive to the needs of a diverse student population.

2

What Is an Accountability Reform?

The ideas that shape current accountability reform in the United States have been developing for quite some time, evolving through federal policies and legislation over the course of the last 50 years (Cross, 2004). When assessing the effectiveness of accountability-based reform for students who are deaf or hard of hearing, it can be helpful to understand the antecedents to this approach. The purpose of this chapter is first to outline a few of the key events that led up to the current accountability framework. Some of the precursors to accountability-based reform are grounded in increasing the equality of educational opportunities for students from oppressed communities. As a result, the language of the laws was based on concepts of social justice and the role of federal government in local education. Other milestones toward an inclusive accountability framework, one that applies to all students in public education, recognized the needs of individuals with disabilities. Laws and reforms for individuals with disabilities were also grounded in concepts of social justice, but access to quality education in this context was not necessarily defined as inclusion in regular education frameworks. The third type of legislation that led up to accountability-based education reform was strengthening of federal measures to improve educational outcomes. The chapter concludes with a discussion of the three main elements of current accountability-based reforms: standards, assessment, and consequences.

Evolution of Accountability in Education

The purpose of this first section is to provide some historical context for accountability legislation. This history covers civil rights legislation, federal funding for children living in poverty, standards-based reform, inclusion of students with disabilities, and reports of student progress. Through each of these reforms, elements of the current accountability framework emerged with the stated goal closing the achievement gaps between (a) the rich and poor, (b) schools with enriched curriculum and those with poor instruction, and (c) students with and without disabilities. Accountability reform, therefore, has roots in issues of equity and the need to improve educational opportunities for whole groups of students. The needs of students who are deaf or hard of hearing have not been explicitly a part of many of these events, but their inclusion in today's accountability reforms is shaped by the previous principles and actions on a national level.

Elementary and Secondary Education Act

In 1965, President Lyndon B. Johnson signed into law the Elementary and Secondary Education Act (ESEA, Pub. L. 89-750), one of many education initiatives during his presidency. ESEA was part of President Johnson's broader "War on Poverty," an important motivator for the law. Before ESEA, the federal government had very little financial input into public education. As a result, states maintained almost exclusive control over the curriculum and instruction of their students. This law was an extension of the civil rights philosophy because it put into place a financial structure to support the goals of equal education. ESEA recognized that the school systems were not equally funded and that children living in low-income areas could not, without additional resources, have an equal education to their more wealthy peers. More specifically, Title I, Part A of ESEA was the first federal initiative to provide funding for students from disadvantaged backgrounds.

ESEA is important because it represents an investment of *federal* dollars into *local* education. The U.S. Congress reauthorizes ESEA on a periodic basis, providing an opportunity for each administration to shape the law. In its early phases, ESEA did not come with "strings attached" as an accountability reform. But with financial contribution comes a sense of responsibility for those expenditures, or at least a right to set criteria to receive federal funds. The George W. Bush administration reauthorized ESEA as the No Child Left Behind Act of 2001 (NCLB). NCLB was not, therefore, developed as its own policy. As a successor to ESEA, NCLB has in its history the goal to close achievement gaps through targeted funding for schools and districts with students living in poverty. The language in NCLB is focused on how to *leverage* the federal funds to implement an accountability system with standards, achievement tests, school report cards, and consequences for schools and districts. Although a focus on achievement gaps is consistent with the original intent of ESEA, NCLB takes the initial principles of a War on Poverty and uses them to create an accountability framework that encompasses the entire public education system. As a result, a national agenda to provide targeted assistance for low-income school districts has transitioned into a mechanism for measuring student proficiency in all schools and districts.

Minimum Competency Standards

Accountability reform, as a national initiative, relies on a stated set of achievement standards that all students should meet as a result of their time in public schools. An early precursor to the later standards-based movement was the Minimum Competency Standards of the 1970s. The purpose of the Minimum Competency Standards was to ensure that every student came away from public education with a set of basic skills and knowledge needed to succeed in the workforce (Gallagher, 1979). Or, at the very least, the hope was to measure who met those standards and who did not. This reform did not have a sustained, significant impact on students or schools. Many students failed to meet these minimum standards set by states, but very few faced consequences such as denial of a high school diploma. In essence, states "blinked" when students were poised to fail within the system (Hess, 2003). The standards were not implemented in a way that created meaningful change for students, teachers, or schools. What the Minimum Competency Standards initiative did demonstrate is how difficult it is to enforce consequences when students do not meet stated goals and objectives. Part of this challenge is the great range of occupational goals within the high school student body. On the one hand, if there are meaningful standards that are challenging enough to prepare students for college, there will be some students who do not meet these standards and thus be designated as "not performing." On the other hand, if standards are too minimal, or do not represent a set of skills required to enter the workforce after high school, then there is no way to determine whether there are schools that are in need of change to ensure equal opportunity for their students. This challenge continues today: deciding how to address schools with students who under-perform, a status based on policy guidelines, is an essential component of accountability reform (Hess, 2006).

A Nation at Risk

Education in the United States is both a local and national process. Student success is seen in a school's high school graduation rate or in the communities' ability to prepare their youth for the workforce. Because funding and curriculum decisions are historically predominantly a state and local issue, this view of educational progress is not surprising. A national sense of the "status," or quality, of education is really only a more recent phenomenon, starting within the last quarter century. *A Nation at Risk* (National Commission on Excellence in Education, 1983) was a landmark report on the status of public education in the United States. The report was an early attempt to describe academic achievement of the nation's public school students. As the title implies, the national findings about public education were not optimistic: American students were largely unprepared in core academic areas, which raised some alarm at both local and national arenas.

In an effort to help leaders be proactive in meeting the challenges found in the report, the *Nation at Risk* report made some key recommendations for improving America's schools. These recommendations represented the first national enumeration of educational goals:

- Strengthen course requirements for high school graduation
- Adopt higher standards of academic performance
- Adopt measurable standards of academic performance
- Increase instructional time
- Raise standards for teachers

The *Nation At Risk* recommendations for improving student achievement focused on many of the elements now a part of NCLB. Until this point, the federal priorities were on providing equal access and resources for schools.

A Nation at Risk was published in the shift toward a focus on standards at all levels, including high school graduation. What the schools taught or how they determined who was ready for high school graduation remained in local control. *A Nation at Risk* brought the question of the goals of education out of the districts and schools and into the national spotlight. The emphasis on *measurable* standards, although small in the scope of the *Nation at Risk* report, paved the way for later legislation that requires assessment as part of education reform (Popham, 2004). The measurable standards piece here foreshadowed the large-scale assessment requirements that are now the centerpiece of accountability reform (discussed in depth in Chapter 4).

Not all of the recommendations in *Nation at Risk* have carried forward with equal weight into accountability reforms. In contrast with recommendations for standards and measures, the recommendation to increase instructional time is largely missing from current accountability measures. Instead, the standards, assessment, and consequences components are assumed to create the climate in which instruction and learning change toward better student outcomes. There is no research that supports this assumption, nor do we have an understanding of the direct and indirect factors that leverage this kind of change. For example, when a school is sanctioned for low student performance, do teachers tailor their instructional approaches to student needs or do students become more highly engaged in the classroom activities? Although the purpose of accountability reform is to close the achievement gap, there is little information about how the changes under this framework will bring about this change within the classroom. We will return to this missing element of instruction in our later discussion of how accountability reforms may or may not be able leverage significant changes in student performance.

Improving America's Schools Act of 1994

Ten years after the *Nation at Risk* report, Congress revised the ESEA provisions to include many of the recommendations from that national commission (Improving America's Schools Act of 1994). The critical change in this reauthorization was that states had to meet reporting criteria to be eligible for federal funding under Title I. States were not held accountable for student outcomes on assessments, but states were required to establish assessment systems for student achievement. More specifically, states were now required to adopt challenging content standards (e.g., what students were expected to know), to set proficiency standards (e.g., determine a "passing" score), and to develop an assessment system. For assessments, states were required to test students in three grades, once in each grade range: Grades 3–5 (elementary), 6–9 (middle school), and 10–12 (high school). These changes were significant in the history of ESEA and reflect the standards-based reform climate of that time period.

These stipulations look very similar to what we see later in NCLB accountability reform. What happened in this earlier version of accountability? States, by and large, did begin to look at their content standards and identify what goals and objectives students should learn. Before this period, some states had content standards, but they were not a transparent, thorough set of content area goals and objectives. For example, standards were not necessarily published on state Web sites for public review, and they consisted of general statements about goals across multiple grade spans. States now were encouraged to be more concrete in their expectations for students in core content areas. In terms of measurement, states also began to implement large-scale standardized testing in at least three grades. These efforts to respond to new requirements took a few years to develop and implement across the country. The accountability components, such as the definitions of proficiency and adequate yearly progress (AYP), were largely cosmetic and consequently fell to a similar fate as the Minimum Competency Standards from two decades earlier. The *Nation at Risk* findings had predicted that there were more than a handful of schools that required significant change to improve student outcomes. In reality, very few schools were required to take corrective action, and when they did, there was a protest from the public. The effectiveness of this accountability reform was limited because the strength of it lay in establishing content standards rather than in measuring student achievement.

Section 504 of the Rehabilitation Act of 1973

The first four events in this chapter pertain primarily to students in regular education, without an emphasis on the structures or outcomes for students with disabilities. Yet there are several precursors to the current accountability framework that addressed issues specific to individuals with disabilities, including students who are deaf or hard of hearing. A precedent to later legislation such as the Americans With Disabilities Act of 1990, the Rehabilitation Act of 1973 prohibited discrimination by federal agencies and by federally funded programs. Following the lead of reforms such as those initiated by *Brown v. the Board of Education of Topeka,* the Rehabilitation Act was passed during the civil rights era and reflects the focus on access and inclusive participation in publicly funded institutions. Because most school districts in the country receive federal aid, Section 504 of the Rehabilitation Act effectively covers all students in public education from discrimination or limited access to services on the basis of a disability. Section 504 has a broad definition of disability:

> Under this law, individuals with disabilities are defined as persons with a physical or mental impairment which substantially limits one or more major life activities. People who have a history of, or who are regarded as having a physical or mental impairment that substantially limits one or more major life activities, are also covered. Major life activities include caring for one's self, walking, seeing, hearing, speaking, breathing, working, performing manual tasks, and learning. Some examples of impairments which may substantially limit major life activities, even with the help of medication or aids/devices, are: AIDS, alcoholism, blindness or visual impairment, cancer, deafness or hearing impairment, diabetes, drug addiction, heart disease, and mental illness. (U.S. Department of Health and Human Services, n.d.)

Applied to schools, Section 504 requires schools and districts to provide necessary accommodations for students with disabilities. Adequate access to curriculum is the central issue when a school or district is asked to provide services to a student with a disability. Access may look quite different for students with different disabilities. For students who are deaf or hard of hearing, access can be interpreted to mean effective communication between the student and teacher and, far less often, between the student and peers. For example, resources such as an interpreter or note taker can help provide access to classroom instruction. The Rehabilitation Act does not require that the student be designated as a special education student to receive these services, nor does it require the district to pay for these services. In this way, the Rehabilitation Act is a less codified legislation than other avenues for receiving accommodations in public schools. Social justice and access to resources for individuals with disabilities were the driving factors behind the Rehabilitation Act. The long-term impact of the Rehabilitation Act was, in part, to put language into place that incorporates students with disabilities into larger educational reforms.

Americans With Disabilities Act

The Americans With Disabilities Act of 1990, or ADA, is a civil rights act that makes it illegal to discriminate against individuals on the basis of their disability. ADA has an even broader definition of the kinds of disabilities that fall under its jurisdiction than the Rehabilitation Act. ADA protects all individuals who have a "physical or mental impairment that substantially limits one or more major life activities, a person who has a history or record of such impairment, or a person who is perceived by others as having an impairment" (U.S. Department of Justice, 2005, p. 1). The goal of this legislation is to provide an opportunity for individuals with disabilities to access and participate in civic life on a basis equal to those without disabilities. As a publicly funded institution, public schools are a part of that civic life.

For some people who view deafness as membership in a culture and not a handicap, ADA designation of deafness as a disability is viewed with open disapproval (Lane, 1999). For example, those individuals who identify with the Deaf community (with a capital *D*) do not consider deafness as an impairment to be thought of as a disability. In a cultural construction of Deaf identity, deafness is a group membership with its own language, organizations, and cultural norms. The legislation does not make the distinction between individuals who are hard of hearing, those who may use amplification to participate in the hearing world, and those who are Deaf and a part of a cultural community. This disagreement about federal definitions and cultural identity continues to be an undercurrent in how students who are deaf or hard of hearing experience national accountability reforms. We will return to this issue later in the book. Definitions aside, people who are deaf or hard of hearing are protected by ADA in their interactions with state and local government; in their place of employment, working with businesses, transportation, telecommunications; and most relevant to our discussion here, in schools.

Individuals With Disabilities Education Act

The Individuals With Disabilities Education Act (IDEA) is the most significant federal special education legislation in place today. IDEA first began in 1990 as a revision of the Education of the Handicapped Act (Pub. L. 94-142) and went through revisions in 1991, 1997, and 2004. IDEA defines eligibility for special education services as having one of 13 disabilities, including "hearing impairment." IDEA differs from the Rehabilitation Act in two key ways. First, the purpose of IDEA is to ensure that students with disabilities have a "free and appropriate public education," often referred to as FAPE, which means that students do not have to pay to receive services that are needed to gain access to the benefits of education. The Rehabilitation Act identified the need for schools to provide services, but did not require districts to pay for those services. IDEA provides parents with recourse to have needed accommodations, tutors, or interpreters as a free part of their student's public education. Second, students with disabilities are to be served in the "least restrictive environment," or LRE. The goal of this provision is to encourage schools and districts to provide as much access to general education curriculum, instruction, and environment as possible. The Rehabilitation Act has far fewer implications on placement decisions than IDEA. The definition of LRE is deliberately vague; the purpose is not to dictate a one-size-fits-all approach for students with disabilities (Zinkil & Gilbert, 2000). For example, the LRE for students who are deaf or hard of hearing may vary depending on the student's linguistic background, cultural group membership, and proximity to different specialized schools or programs (Eccarius, 1997). Take, for example, a case of a Deaf student who does not use American Sign Language or English because the family's first language is spoken Spanish. If there is a specialized program for students who are deaf or hard of hearing who come from homes where English is not the native language, even if further away than the local neighborhood school, then that setting may be a LRE for the student. Yet, as discussed in Chapter 2, LRE provisions under IDEA have contributed to the shift in student placement into regular education settings and away from separate programs for students who are deaf or hard of hearing.

Although early versions of IDEA gave students with disabilities the right to a free and appropriate education, it did not stipulate to what standards they be educated and how the school systems should report academic progress. Policies and practices to include students with disabilities into accountability frameworks have become increasingly formalized and regulated by IDEA over the last two decades (McGrew, Thurlow, Shriner, & Spiegel, 1992). The 1997 reauthorization of IDEA required states to include students with disabilities in state and local assessments, with appropriate accommodations, if needed. Instead of focusing primarily on the individual's *access* to education, the reauthorized IDEA showed a concern for the *academic success* of individuals with disabilities (National Center on Educational Outcomes, 1998). The 2004 revision (Individuals With Disabilities Education Improvement Act) aligns the assessment process with the accountability framework of NCLB. The new IDEA thus reflects a shift in thinking: educators are now asked to define what standards are used to evaluate students with disabilities and to report on resulting student achievement (Wilmshurst & Brue, 2005; Wright & Wright, 2005).

The intent of IDEA is to provide increased access and accountability for students with disabilities, including students who are deaf or hard of hearing. However, there may be some implications of IDEA that actually limit access to an LRE (Siegel, 2005). Siegel points out that access is through communication with both teachers and peers. Siegel turns to the U.S. Constitution and the first amendment guarantee of freedom of speech, or freedom of communication, as an overlooked aspect of the placement debate. Although not prescribed in the law, IDEA has shifted student enrollment away from regional programs or schools for the deaf toward regular education settings. Without teachers, interpreters, and peers who use the child's language, do students who are deaf have access to communication? When a school is held accountable for student progress, there may need to be some consideration of the language and communication resources available to the student. We will return to this central question in later chapters that discuss use of accommodations and access to quality education goals of accountability reform.

No Child Left Behind Act of 2001

The No Child Left Behind Act of 2001 (NCLB) was the sixth reauthorization of ESEA. Easily the most controversial educational measure in recent years, NCLB was signed into law on January 8, 2002. At its heart, the purpose of NCLB flows from its predecessors (Hess & Petrilli, 2006). The statement of purpose gives the overall goal of this legislation: "The purpose of this title is to ensure that all children have a fair, equal, and significant opportunity to obtain a high-quality education and reach, at a minimum, proficiency on challenging state academic achievement standards and state academic assessments." The method by which this goal is met, however, reflects the growing shift away from equity in *access* to education toward equity in *education outcomes*. The premise behind NCLB is that education for students in Title I schools will be improved if there are (a) clear expectations of educational goals, (b) measurement of student progress, and (c) consequences for schools and districts that do not meet educational goals. The assumption is that financial resources provided through Title I funds are necessary, but not sufficient to close achievement gaps.

The Accountability Reform Framework

NCLB is one example of an overall approach to education policy: accountability-based reform. NCLB's reform approach emphasizes the consequences for low levels of student achievement in hopes to motivate effective change within classrooms and schools. Whether accountability as a concept can close the achievement gap depends as much on the strength of the theory of accountability as it does on its ability to be implemented across diverse settings (McDonnell, 2005). Accountability relies on external motivators to encourage teachers and students to change behaviors. NCLB's version of accountability assumes that the best way to create change is through a set of consequences for schools that fail to meet progress goals. In reality, accountability is popular as an idea, but very difficult to achieve (Moe, 2003). Academic achievement rests within students; students are the only ones who can provide evidence of whether or not they have learned. How well learning is measured is critical to the integrity of accountability. The effectiveness of accountability therefore relies on (a) how well it leverages change in instructional practice and learning and (b) and how accurately it measures learning outcomes for students.

When looking at the feasibility of accountability provisions, especially for students who are deaf or hard of hearing, it is important to look at the individual components of accountability reform (Palmer & Coleman, 2004). As illustrated in the previous section, the elements of an accountability system have arisen in response to different "eras" of civil rights and standards-based reforms. The framework of accountability rests on three main pillars: standards, assessment, and consequences. Standards and assessments are carryovers from previous educational reforms; consequences are a newly added measure directed at improving student outcomes. Figure 2.1 gives an overview of how these three components work together with classroom instruction as well as with other student and school factors. The discussion that follows considers each component with potential considerations for students who are deaf or hard of hearing.

Starting at the top of Figure 2.1, academic standards articulate the content knowledge that states want students to learn (and teachers to teach). These standards are determined state by state and, as a result, vary greatly across the country. Unlike many other countries, the United States does not have a national curriculum that applies to all students. What a student must learn to be successful on tests of academic achievement differs by states across the country. The standards component of educational reform pushes issues of curriculum content to the center of policy discussions (Barton, 2006).

The shift in focus to curricular content has also been especially strong in deaf education. In his address to the International Congress on the Education of the Deaf, Moores (1991) situated the question of *what* to teach deaf students in the context of two other pressing questions in deaf education: *Where* and *how* should deaf students be taught? These three questions are linked in ways that are not salient for students in regular education. Where the student is taught and what language (or languages) or methods are used in instruction influence curriculum decisions. The special needs of students who are deaf or hard of hearing require not only professionals trained in deaf education but also interpreters, supplemental time spent on language skills, and classroom environments that sometimes include students with multiple disabilities. Much of the discussion around curriculum is a matter of time and sequence. Students who are deaf or hard of hearing often need additional

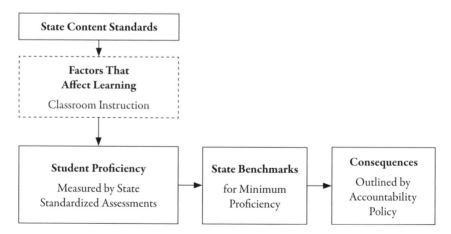

Figure 2.1. Components of current accountability framework.

time to establish essential language skills before incorporating extensive literacy and content area curriculum. The challenge is to incorporate these demands into teaching subject matter, on grade level, proposed by external state and federal agencies. The push for high standards for all students, including students who are deaf or hard of hearing, will challenge administrators and teachers to juggle traditional curriculum in programs for students who are deaf or hard of hearing (such as speech, sign language, auditory training) with content-specific matter such as reading, math, and science (Moores, 1991). Moores concluded that "very soon, we will have to establish priorities in the education of the deaf. . . . [W]e will have to develop a judicious mix of special and general methods and materials to enable deaf children to develop to the best of their potential. . . ." (Moores, 1991, p. 37). Even nearly two decades later, these words still ring true. Accountability reform may very well create additional pressure toward a greater emphasis on grade-level content standards for students who are deaf or hard of hearing.

This call for priorities in deaf education brings up an important philosophical stance about the goals of special education: Special education should develop educational goals and priorities that are based on the needs of its population. The logical connection is easy to draw. Those charged with the education of students with disabilities should be trained in and practice the best methods and content for students' academic development. For students who are deaf or hard of hearing, the deaf educators, administrators, and parents would have the greatest insight as to the necessary and reasonable sequence of curriculum goals for their students. In this light, accountability reform could be interpreted as a catalyst for special education to raise the expectations it has for students who are deaf or hard of hearing. Although both fields may establish standards for students who are deaf or hard of hearing, which set holds priority depends on whether there is enough flexibility within larger educational reform for specific goals. For example, given what we know about the challenges in literacy development for students who are deaf or hard of hearing, would it be possible to set a longer time frame for reaching regular education grade-level proficiency in reading? When standards are the result of a dialogue between the community of those teaching students who are deaf or hard of hearing and state or federal policymakers, it may be possible to gain some flexibility in how curricular content is conceptualized within accountability reform.

Assessment represents how states will measure what students have learned. As with academic content standards, the breadth of knowledge that is tested by states' large-scale assessments varies greatly. Until quite recently, there were very few publicly available mechanisms in place that could measure successful learning. There were neither public reports of student proficiency nor ways to identify whether individual teachers were successful in educating their students. On a very local level, this lack is particularly apparent for the individual student. Individual student report cards are based on classroom assessments and not reported to anyone outside of the student and her parents. Exceptions include some school-level reporting of student grades in New York (Allington & McGill-Franzen, 1992) and Texas (Bernal & Valencia, 2000). National assessments such as National Assessment of Educational Progress have tracked overall student performance, yet results cannot be traced back to individual students, teachers, or schools. As a result, there has been little transparency in the assessment process, making it next to impossible to know whether teachers were teaching effectively and whether students were learning content standards.

In a break from the past, student test scores have become a foundational component of current accountability reforms. In a sense, student test scores are used as the key indicator of success or failure for large-scale education policy. Although using assessment as the driving force for reform may seem to be "putting the cart before the horse," student achievement data are still being used as indicators for where standards and reforms are needed (Barton, 2006). Test scores can provide important information about effects of reforms on student achievement, but quality assessment is a very difficult process. Haertel (1999) notes that there are many unproven assumptions driving the use of educational accountability for standards-based reforms:

> If the standards are appropriate, if students and teachers are prepared to accept the challenge of meeting them, if the phase-in period for accountability is realistic, if reliable and valid tests are available to ascertain the extent of students' mastery, if teachers have the requisite knowledge and training to help students meet the challenge of new standards, if schools are not hobbled by extraneous demands and requirements, if necessary instructional materials and resources are available, if out-of-school factors are given appropriate consideration . . . then a measurement-driven accountability system ought to show just which

students are working and which ones are slacking off, which teachers and schools should be rewarded and which ones should be punished. (p. 662)

Effective assessment faces large challenges under accountability reform (Newmann & Wehlage, 1995). The first challenge is that student learning can be difficult to measure using a standardized test (Moe, 2003). When differences in test scores are due to construct *relevant* variance, then those differences reflect accurate measurement of variations in student knowledge. Factors such as student motivation and how the test items are constructed can create what is called "construct irrelevant variance." This scenario results in test scores that may be different, not due to the level of student proficiency, but due to factors that should not be measured in the testing process. Assessment development is a highly technical process that requires careful attention to issues of validity and reliability. Validity refers to the extent that the test measures what the student knows (Barton, 2006). Threats to validity include poorly worded questions or items that do not align with the content on the state standards. Reliability refers to the extent that a person taking the same test twice (i.e., without additional instruction or test preparation) will receive a similar score. A reliable test score is one that is stable, at least within a short time frame. Using principles of validity and reliability, states are required to demonstrate that their assessments are of high quality and can be trusted to represent the knowledge and skills of their students.

There are many critics of standardized tests (Cuban, 2004; Smith, Miller-Kahn, Heinecke, & Jarvis, 2004). For example, there can be bias in the items against students from culturally and linguistically diverse backgrounds, teachers may limit their instruction to the material on test items, or standardized tests may measure memorized facts more than higher order thinking (Heubert & Hauser, 1999). Issues of bias apply as much, if not more so, to students who are deaf or hard of hearing (Gordon & Stump, 1996; Luckner & Bowen, 2006; Lollis & LaSasso, 2009). For example, test items that refer to music or sound or experiences requiring the ability to hear would be biased against a student with hearing loss. Concerns about the accuracy of standardized tests increase when they are high-stakes tests (Clarke, Haney, Madaus, Lynch, & Lynch, 2000; De Stefano & Metzer, 1991; Gratz, 2000). High-stakes tests are those where results are used to grant access to a program (e.g., college admission) or degree completion (e.g., high school graduation).

The accuracy and integrity of these tests is particularly important because decisions based on their results have great significance in the lives of students who take them. A more complete discussion on the use of high-stakes assessment for students who are deaf or hard of hearing in accountability reform is provided in Chapter 4.

Consequences are the set of rewards and sanctions that follow from student performance on assessments. Depending on the accountability system, consequences can include not only rewards for strong performance but also changes that must be made in response to poor performance. Some examples of consequences that reward a school may be official recognition as a "School of Excellence," bonus pay for teachers, or increased independence or flexibility in administrative decision making. Negative consequences for schools that are viewed as in need of improvement can come in the form of reduced funding but are more likely to result in sanctions such as increased monitoring and less flexibility in instruction (Cuban, 2004).

Perhaps the greatest change under accountability reform is that of instituting the system of consequences that comes with an accountability framework (Education Commission of the States, 2004). In contrast with the standards and assessment components that have significant variability from state to state, consequences under federal accountability policies are standardized and implemented in a similar sequence across the country. Because consequence elements can involve parents in the accountability framework, they are salient to the voting public and take on added significance. Although consequences are just one piece of the whole process, many critics of NCLB focus on the consequences schools face for not meeting performance guidelines (Abernathy, 2007). The consequences element, in particular, takes what was originally civil rights legislation to provide more resources for low-income students and puts the emphasis on how schools can boost test scores to avoid sanctions or even closure. The choice to have consequences is not necessarily divergent from the original purpose of ESEA, but the chosen criteria, time frame, and specific sanctions are radically different from the law's original intent. In an effort to close achievement gaps, policymakers have changed the motivation behind ESEA from one of increased access for a relative few— impoverished students—to one of evaluation of all students that determines states' eligibility for the Title I funds. Whether or not the change to a system of accountability results in closing the achievement gaps for underserved students remains to be seen.

In a sense, federal accountability helps states make difficult decisions about consequences that schools and districts face when students do not show adequate levels of proficiency in core content areas. The Minimum Content Standards era demonstrated how challenging it is to implement consequences when students or schools do not perform to the target levels. Although early phases of sanctions under NCLB come in the form of additional resources (e.g., tutoring) for students and choices for parents, the ultimate consequence for schools is to face restructuring and, ultimately, closure. This form of consequence is a significant increase in the level of control exerted by federal law, by means of the states, over local school administration. In a high-stakes environment, particularly one in which control over the results can be out of the hands of those being held accountable, questions of the fairness of accountability measures will only intensify in the coming years. How these issues affect students who are deaf or hard of hearing are explored in greater depth in Chapter 5.

Conclusion

The trajectory of events that laid groundwork for future accountability policies in public education in the United States represent a shift from access to outcomes—from separate policies for students with disabilities to an integrated, national plan. The *Brown v. the Board of Education of Topeka* Supreme Court decision over 50 years ago ushered in an era of civil rights, bringing a purpose and language to those who were concerned about unequal access to education for students who had been intentionally kept away from the mainstream curriculum. This focus on access to education carries through much of the legislation reviewed in this chapter. Access can take on different meanings in a discussion of education for students who are deaf or hard of hearing. A series of legislation, specifically the Rehabilitation Act and IDEA, provide a legal framework for questions of limited access for individuals with disabilities in the workplace and in schools. These laws largely assume that "access" equals participation in regular education settings to the largest extent practicable. Under this assumption, a "restrictive environment" can be interpreted as meaning locations and context that are different from where and how the majority of students learn. Schools for the deaf or programs that organize students in a context separate from their hearing peers offer an alternative way of viewing "access." In this context, "access" relates to the accessibility of the curricular content, not the physical location where instruction occurs. Yet accountability reforms raise the bar, so to speak, from access to production of learning outcomes. *Student performance is the new metric by which "access" is measured.* The emphasis thus shifts away from whether students with disabilities participate in the physical environment of regular education to how well they learn content area standards. For those who support separate schools for the deaf or programs for students who are hard of hearing, this shift may be a welcomed one.

*   *   *

The next four chapters will delve into many of these issues in greater detail. Each chapter addresses what structures serve students who are deaf or hard of hearing and a more specific question of how accountability affects them. The role of accountability in closing achievement gaps takes on different implications in each of these chapters. Public education is a broad entity with many players; there are differences, in particular, in who or what institution is being held accountable in different components of accountability-based reform. Depending on the lens, accountability may apply to the school for the deaf, the district that houses a program for students who are deaf or hard of hearing, or the higher education teacher preparation programs that credential the teachers who serve this student population. For example, Chapter 6 looks at the accountability reform measures that focus on teacher preparation and certification. Teachers are essential agents in improving student achievement. Therefore, just as schools are held accountable for student outcomes, states are held accountable for teacher credentials. Students who are deaf or hard of hearing make up a diverse student group that is served by professionals with a wide variety of backgrounds across several different educational settings. The broader discussions of accountability, or accountability in special education, will take on specific meaning when looking at how it applies to the public education of students who are deaf or hard of hearing.

3

What Does Accountability Measure?

Whereas Chapter 2 gave an overview of the main components of account-ability reform, this chapter focuses specifically on the construct of content standards. Curricular standards drive both the content of instruction and, important when looking at accountability reform, the content of assessment. The purpose of this chapter is to review the literature on content area stan-dards and to raise important issues that may apply to students who are deaf or hard of hearing.

Content Standards: What Is Tested?

Since the 1994 authorization of ESEA, states have been urged to develop rig-orous content standards for their students in core content areas. By focusing assessment on core content areas, accountability reform has only increased the importance of a clearly articulated, standards-based curriculum (Hess, 2003). For example, at the start of NCLB, only math and reading were as-sessed in the required grades. In 2007, states added science to the state assess-ments in selected grades. Although states are allowed to test other content areas such as social studies, much of the discussion regarding assessment for accountability purposes has been limited to math and reading subject areas. In the context of education for students who are deaf or hard of hearing, standards for reading play a prominent role. As discussed in Chapter 1, the achievement gap between students who are deaf or hard of hearing and their peers has been greater for reading than for math. Reading is also intimately tied to language, and some students who are deaf or hard of hearing have a very different language and communication background from children without a hearing loss.

Several national agencies have put forth standards, guidelines, and objectives for literacy achievement in the elementary grades (e.g., National Assessment of Educational Progress, 2000; National Reading Panel, 2000). The current move in national reading policy is to emphasize decoding strategies in reading instruction. The National Reading Panel (2000) reviewed 100,000 studies on how students learn to read. The panel concluded that

> [e]ffective reading instruction includes teaching children to break apart and manipulate the sounds in words (phonemic awareness), teaching them that these sounds are represented by letters of the alphabet which can then be blended together to form words (phonics), having them practice what they have learned by reading aloud with guidance and feedback (guided oral reading), and applying reading comprehension strategies to guide and improve reading comprehension. (p. 10)

The National Reading Panel standards for reading achievement and assessment provide an example of priorities that have been put into place for all students in public education, including students with disabilities and English Language Learners. Thompson, Johnstone, Thurlow, and Clapper (2004) analyzed, in depth, the content of state standards for literacy. This analysis found that states focused not only on basic skill acquisition but also on knowledge of the conventions of written language, how reading can be an interactive, higher order thinking activity, how to problem solve, and reading as a catalyst for personal growth. Under current accountability reforms, each state develops and defines its own standards in the core content areas. (Work is under way to develop a Common Core of State Standards that would bring together state expectations for student academic progress.) A complete list of links to current state standards documents can be found on the National Center for Education Outcomes Web site: http://education

---

Phonics and Word Recognition: Kindergarten

0.3.03   Know and apply grade-level phonics and word analysis skills in decoding words.

    a. Demonstrate basic knowledge of one-to-one letter-sound correspondences by producing the primary or many of the most frequent sounds for each consonant.

    b. Associate the long and short sounds with common spellings (graphemes) for the five major vowels.

    c. Read common high-frequency words by sight (e.g., *the, of, to, you, she, my, is, are, do, does*).

    d. Distinguish between similarly spelled words by identifying the sounds of the letters that differ.

Note. From Minnesota State Department of Education, 2010, *2010 Minnesota Academic Standards in English Language Arts K–12*, p. 26, Roseville, MN: Author. Retrieved from http://education.state.mn.us/MDE/Academic_Excellence/Academic_Standards/index.html

---

Box 3.1. Minnesota Academic Standards in English Language Arts K–12 for Word Recognition for Kindergarten

.umn.edu/nceo/). The Minnesota State Department of Education gives an excellent example of how states have drawn on the National Reading Panel report to establish their own standards for reading. Minnesota has literacy development standards and benchmarks, by literacy skill, for each grade in K–8 and collectively for Grades 9–12. For example, students at the end of their kindergarten year are to have acquired the word recognition skills outlined in Box 3.1.

The Minnesota example gives a clear outline of word recognition goals for students entering first grade. This list also closely resembles recommendations from the National Reading Panel, with a focus on *phonetics and decoding* as tools for developing word recognition and reading fluency. Other literacy skills, including comprehension and engaging in diverse types of literature, are also included on the state standards. This set of objectives can largely be measured with student demonstration of reading skills (see Kame'enui, Fuchs, Francis, Good, O'Connor, Simmons et al., 2006, for a review of assessment strategies for standards-based literacy skills). Content standards at each grade level thus play a large role in instructional practice in reading, particularly in the early grades.

Do the conclusions of the National Reading Panel and state standards for literacy apply to research findings about literacy development in students who are deaf or hard of hearing? Deaf education, as a field, has sustained a lively discourse on the primacy of auditory-based skills, and thus phonemic awareness, with students who cannot hear those sounds. As discussed in Chapter 1, literacy instruction has followed (at least) two different lines of thought in deaf education: a "top-down" approach, focusing on an embedded, holistic language strategy, and a "bottom-up" approach that emphasizes phonetics, letter-sound matching, and decoding. Schirmer and McGough (2005) provide a thorough discussion of the relevance of the National Reading Panel recommendations for students who are deaf or hard of hearing. In this analysis, Schirmer and McGough outline the key components of the National Reading Panel report: Phonemic awareness and phonics instruction, fluency, vocabulary development and text comprehension, and the use of computer technology in reading instruction. The authors found that the research in the deaf education literature focuses primarily on *descriptions* of reading strategies and skills and not on the *efficacy* of different instructional approaches. For example, the research base demonstrates that some deaf students can and do use phonological coding in their reading. However, it is not clear whether this ability is a *predictor* of proficient reading or a skill that is acquired during or after literacy development. As a result, it is challenging to know what interventions to increase literacy are most appropriate for students who are deaf or hard of hearing.

Defining *Proficiency*

What are we holding states, districts, and schools accountable for? In any accountability reform, student progress needs to be evaluated against some type of goal or rubric. NCLB asked states to develop a set of proficiency standards, with at least three categories: basic, proficient, and advanced. Although all states must establish these proficiency standards, the definitions for these categories are left to the states (Barton, 2006; Linn, 2003b). Historical factors in each state differ, which leads to a wide variety of standards and expectations for student achievement (McDermott, 2003). State determinations of what qualifies as proficiency, or not, is a critical component in our overall understanding of student achievement (Linn, 2003a, 2003b). Schools in rigorous states will have far fewer students meet proficiency standards than those in less rigorous states (Kingsbury, Olson, Cronin, Hauser, & Houser, 2004).

On the flip side, states with lenient standards may understate what students actually need to be proficient and meet the demands of the workplace or postsecondary education.

There does appear to be some consensus building, however, on percentile scores that count as "proficient." States seem to cluster at the 30th percentile for proficiency in third-grade reading and the 35th percentile for eighth-grade reading (Kingsbury et al., 2004). In other words, if a third-grade student performs better than 30% of her peers, her work is rated as "proficient." The shift upward from 30th percentile to 35th percentile can be problematic when students who score at a "proficient" cut point in elementary school are later seen as failing to meet these levels in middle school. Low proficiency standards in elementary school can leave students, parents, and teachers unprepared for more rigorous standards in the upper grades. When schools are evaluated on the performance of their students, there should at least be a reasonable comparison in the relative difficulty and definitions of proficiency scores between grades (Kingsbury et al., 2004; Linn, 2005b). This attempt to make scores comparable allows elementary, middle, and high schools equal chance at achieving satisfactory ratings based on student test scores.

How does this "calibration gap" between grades affect the test scores of students who are deaf or hard of hearing? As discussed in Chapter 2, the achievement gaps between students who are deaf or hard of hearing and their peers who can hear have widened as students have progressed from elementary school to middle school. In other words, as students move into the upper grades, students who are deaf or hard of hearing make less progress, per year, than their peers who can hear. If the standards for meeting proficiency also rise, there may be a potential drop-off in the number of students who are deaf or hard of hearing who can meet state proficiency standards, which will affect those students' eligibility for high school diplomas and ability to transition into postsecondary education or occupational opportunities.

The calibration gap can also affect educational settings for students who are deaf or hard of hearing. In elementary grades, students who are deaf or hard of hearing are more likely to attend their local schools than students in the upper grades who are deaf or hard of hearing. Schools for the deaf, which have seen a shift toward enrollment in the upper grades, are accountable for the performance of middle and high school students. If there is a calibration gap, or more challenging proficiency standards for their students in upper grades, then schools for the deaf will be subject to stricter criteria for success than the elementary schools. They may, as a result, face greater sanctions within an accountability framework than if the proficiency standards were equitable across grade ranges.

Cohort Versus Growth Models

Part of the challenge in quantifying proficiency is differences in measurement models used in accountability reform. In a cohort approach to measuring student proficiency, students in each participating grade are tested to give a "percent proficient" score for that grade. For example, scores for fourth graders are tested in 2007 and compared with scores for fourth graders tested in 2008. The cohorts of fourth graders are measured against each other; the amount of progress individual students made in either year is not taken into account.

The cohort model is the most widely used method of assessment during NCLB. However, as of 2007, alternatives to this approach were implemented in a handful of states (U.S. Department of Education, 2007a). These models are referred to as "growth models" or "value-added" approaches to achievement. In principle, these approaches measure gains in student knowledge from one year to the next (Hanushek & Raymond, 2003). Schools are evaluated on the "growth" demonstrated by their students over an annual or biannual time frame. The key difference between this growth approach and the cohort approach is that accountability is based on gains in individual student achievement, that is, based on measures of changes in individual student knowledge (not on a different cohort of students in each grade from year to year). This approach acknowledges the starting point of each student as a contributing factor to the level of proficiency she has at the end of the school year. This approach also makes intuitive sense in that teachers are held accountable for the time frame in which they work with students and not (directly) for what educational progress those students made in previous years.

There are many technical issues to be resolved in using growth models, but they do hold an appeal to those who see the cohort model as punitive to teachers and schools (Barton, 2006; Graham, 2007; Linn, 2005b). For students who are deaf or hard of hearing, there may be some promising options available in an accountability framework that measures gains in student knowledge. For example, if a student comes to elementary education far below grade level in reading, but makes significant progress, the school can promote this improvement as success, even if the student is not reading at grade level at the end of the year. One concern, however, is the reality that students do not make the same rate of progress within the standard calendar year or from one calendar year to the next (Kornhaber & Orfield, 2001). There are developmental spurts and plateaus in learning in all students. Although schools may receive recognition for student progress in a "spurt" year, "plateau" years might reflect poorly on a school, for reasons outside of its teaching effectiveness.

Returning to the historical patterns in achievement levels for students who are deaf or hard of hearing, there tends to be a plateau in achievement gains in the upper grades (Qi & Mitchell, 2007; Traxler, 2000). In a growth model approach to measurement, secondary students who follow this pattern will not demonstrate sufficient gain in knowledge from year to year. This pattern is particularly true when we rely solely on standardized assessments that may not measure other areas of development such as occupational skills or strengths in non-core content areas. It may be useful to look at gains in terms of needed skills instead of in a "grade-level" unit of change. For example, suppose a student has an IEP plan that calls for development of proficiency in algebra to be successful in a postsecondary institution of higher education. Necessary growth for this student may be the attainment of that goal. It is also possible that the student may make some progress but not achieve total proficiency. Measuring growth in terms of concrete goals and progress toward them would require greater specificity in what the student has done than a basic "proficient" versus "not proficient" score on a standardized assessment. In summary, growth models do provide a more individual approach to assessment, but how educational gains are evaluated are critical questions to consider within the context of accountability and students who are deaf or hard of hearing.

Standards are not implemented in a vacuum but, rather, are a part of a larger system that is bringing its values and priorities for literacy education into the landscape (McDonnell, McLaughlin, & Morison, 1997). Over the past decade, content standards for students across the nation have become more detailed and focused on National Reading Panel outcomes. Differences between state standards documents and those found in deaf education may reflect the different priorities of the hearing and deaf literacy research communities. There is also certainly debate within the deaf education community about educational best practices or evidence-based instruction for deaf students (Lytle & Rovins, 1997). However, if educators assume that teachers of students who are deaf or hard of hearing need to focus on a different set of standards to foster literacy development in this population, then deaf education models may emphasize specialized methods and curriculum for their students (Laurent Clerc National Deaf Education Center, 2001). The effectiveness of national accountability reforms rests, in part, on the applicability of the standards to the students learning them. If methods are a critical component of how students who are deaf or hard of hearing learn, then it may be detrimental to focus accountability only on student outcomes and not on the learning process itself.

The potential impact of this absence of teaching and learning from the accountability framework is not unique to students who are deaf or hard of hearing (Hinde, 2003). The point of accountability reforms is not to recommend a policy that prescribes specific teaching methods for different student groups. However, there is currently a fear of harmful emphasis on teaching to the test that measures those standards (Gratz, 2000; Herman & Golan, 1993; Hess & Brigham, 2000; Ketter & Pool, 2001). Moon, Callahan, and Tomlinson (2003) suggest that increases in test scores, absent reform in instruction, is a result of better test skill preparation and not of real increases in student knowledge. In essence, the "black box" between standards to be learned and assessments to measure learning is presumed to be static and universal. At the very least, student progress is presumed to occur at the same rate for all students. In accountability reform, the content of state standards drives curriculum on the front end, whereas the standardized assessments drives instruction from the back end. For students with disabilities or those who come from a linguistically diverse backgrounds, the standards and measurement process may not drive teaching activities in a developmentally appropriate manner.

Recommendations for Action

In this and the next five chapters, I will make recommendations for future action based on the available research literature and policy information. These recommendations draw on the findings described here as well as the principles behind accountability reforms and the needs of students who are deaf or hard of hearing. Recommendations are broken down into three categories: (a) policy, (b) research, and (c) practice. Although there will likely be some overlap between these domains, these categories will assist educators and policymakers in creating a task list for the years ahead. I hope that the recommendations offered here and in the remainder of this book provide a framework for further dialogue on how to best serve students who are deaf or hard of hearing within an accountability framework.

The policy piece of this section relates primarily to the development of state content standards for reading. The Common Core State Standards Initiative might be a suitable place to work on these issues jointly across multiple states. The first recommendation is for policymakers to allow for greater diversity in the information on which the state content standards are based. Instead of using the one-size-fits-all approach to reading standards, it would be helpful to explicitly include *alternate* routes to literacy development in this process. For example, there is a long and rich research tradition in bilingual education and special education. These fields have a research base that offers insight for how to think about reading development for students with disabilities or those who are English Language Learners when those groups reach early elementary grades. The research base and practices from these fields could be explicitly outlined in standards documents and in the evidence used to construct them. This shift would require, at the very least, including representatives from deaf education and other diverse groups when outlining content goals for different age groups. Articulating the potential for multiple routes to literacy proficiency within content standards would lay the groundwork for flexibility in instructional methods and, ultimately, in assessments (see next section of this chapter).

Another concern with the content standards policies is that they are issued for specific grade levels. However, not all students acquire academic skills at the same rate. Students who are deaf or hard of hearing may learn individual components of reading at a later point than their hearing peers. For example, students who do not hear may take more time to develop phonics skills than those students who have had exposure to spoken English throughout their early childhood. The focus on "grade-level" standards is less helpful for those students who are deaf or hard of hearing who are learning to read, particularly in the early grades. Students who are deaf or hard of hearing would benefit from a more flexible time line and sequence of skills, one that allows for developing a student's strengths in order to leverage them to assist in areas that are in need of improvement. In light of this need for developmental milestones that represent overall goals and not age-specific targets, I support a return to *grade-range* standards that were more common before the advent of NCLB.

The second main area of policy recommendations relates to the definitions of *proficiency* in core content areas. States set their individual cut points for proficiency for each tested area and grade. As discussed earlier, these cut points can vary from grade to grade. For accountability to be fair for all schools (elementary compared with middle or high school) or even teachers within a school, it would be necessary to make the cut points for proficiency consistent for each grade. So, for example, if the cut points require that students perform at a 30th percentile to be deemed proficient, then this rubric should be applied to all subject areas and tested grades.

There are some additional considerations, however, to using a percentile to set proficiency rates. A percentile score measures a student's performance compared with his peers. Students are not evaluated on the percentage of problems they got right on the test, but on how well they did relative to the tested cohort. The percentile score thus depends, in part, on how well the other students perform in that subject area. But who are the peers of a student who is deaf or hard of hearing, especially in cases where the student who is deaf or hard of hearing is a single student or one of only a few? If a state is using percentiles to make proficiency cut points, I recommend that states provide percentile data for students who are deaf or hard of hearing, or at the very least, to all students with disabilities. This approach would serve two purposes. First, it would give the deaf education community a sense of how students are performing relative to their peers. The *Stanford Achievement Test-HI* test norms provide some context on a national level, but this test is tied neither to the state content standards nor to the accountability framework. Second, a reference group for either students who are deaf or hard of hearing or students with disability could be used to determine more reasonable *growth* rates, if a state decides to implement a growth model to track proficiency. The current accelerated learning goal of 100% proficiency in less than a decade is not appropriate; a percentile score for students who are deaf or hard of hearing could be used to document where students are relative to their peers and what targets to set for individual schools and districts.

Quality growth models, or value-added assessment systems, will be an integral part of how assessment data meet the needs of an accountability framework as well as individual teachers and parents. This recommendation to consider growth models for students who are deaf or hard of hearing comes with several caveats. Two of those have been stated above: (a) that we return to grade ranges and not individual grade assessments for accountability and (b) that there be an understanding of the student's performance relative to peers who are deaf or hard of hearing, in addition to the student body as a whole. How the change over time is evaluated will, in the end, determine the utility of growth modeling. For example, if a student's overall test score plateaus, one's first conclusion might be that the student did not learn more information over the course of the year. However, the test format is quite limited in how it captures intellectual growth. A growth model must therefore include a third condition, which is to use more than one measure of change. Reliance on a single test for high-stakes decisions is invalid and, at times, unethical. For students who are deaf or hard of hearing, progress may be made in areas that are not captured by a large-scale standardized test. For example, students may show great strides in domains such as American Sign Language or critical thinking, but this improvement would not appear on the state test. Growth models will need to be more inclusive in the kinds of information monitored for their results to be meaningful for teachers and parents.

Several research priorities arise from this discussion. The first is a need for greater information about *how* students who are deaf or hard of hearing learn to read, especially in light of the diversity in backgrounds and achievement outcomes developed by state policymakers. If there is an alternate route to reading, then what does it look like and how do we foster it in a more comprehensive manner? Although this work has been under way for several decades, there is not sufficient evidence to guide specialized instruction for this diverse population. There needs to be an emphasis not only on measuring progress toward the outcomes such as fluency and decoding skills but also on identifying the factors that contribute to different learning trajectories. The deaf education research field has been limited in its construction of language and literacy development models that respond to the diversity of student experiences. More complex models need to include how individual student characteristics, family resources, school setting, and instructional approach interact to result in varying levels of student achievement.

To conduct research involving complex literacy acquisition models, the deaf education research field will need to institute greater collaboration between institutions and perhaps even countries. The low-incidence nature of this population makes gaining adequate numbers of study participants a huge challenge. Although there are several informal "centers" for reading research with students who are deaf or hard of hearing, very little of the research agenda occurs in a coordinated fashion. Deliberate collaboration would improve the power of research designs and increase the ability to include students that represent the diversity within the population of students who are deaf or hard of hearing. Descriptive information such as the educational attainment of students who are deaf or hard of hearing and evaluative research such as the effectiveness of reading interventions are both needed to improve policy and practice for students who are deaf or hard of hearing.

For all of the reach into local education seen by NCLB, instructional practice still remains largely in the hands of classroom teachers and school staff members. The deaf education community might use this reality as an opportunity to conduct some internal assessment of how different instructional strategies in reading prepare students who are deaf or hard of hearing, particularly those components outlined by the National Reading Panel. Although this evaluation may include the large-scale state assessments, data collected should reflect the goals and priorities of the deaf education community. It would be particularly helpful to know for whom different strategies work well and whether strategies are used in combination or alone. The complexity models outlined above also would be useful. Accountability for educational outcomes would thus be internally driven instead of externally mandated, drawing on the professional expertise within each school setting and collecting information that would increase understanding of the effectiveness of literacy instruction for students who are deaf or hard of hearing.

Conclusion

The purpose of this chapter was to provide greater detail on the "what" of accountability reform: What are students expected to learn? Answer: It depends. This conditional response may seem counterintuitive in a framework that seeks to promote consistency in what teachers teach across diverse contexts. The concept of standards in education implies a common target and a shared set of goals for teachers and students. Yet the standards for education under accountability reform are a common experience for students only at a very local level. The first very salient level of variation is at the state level. Each state has its own standards, or at the broadest level, a set of shared standards with a consortium of other states. Within each state, districts can also establish curricula that guide instruction within schools in their district. Within a single grade in a specific school or district, students will take the same exam and likely have very similar instruction. It is within the classroom context where the experiences of students who are deaf or hard of hearing are likely to diverge from their hearing peers.

Accountability policy, as it currently stands, is weakest in its ability to leverage quality classroom instruction to improve student achievement. Even the teacher quality accountability components, as discussed in Chapter 6, do not address classroom instruction. Much of the emphasis in regular education is on outcomes—what students know at the end of each school year. The accountability model does not include consideration of *how* students get to those educational goals, other than the requirement that schools should look for evidence-based practice. This gap in the policy is, I think, an important opportunity for educators who work with students who are deaf or hard of hearing.

4

How Do We Measure Progress?

If one word captures the heart of recent accountability reforms, especially in how NCLB is experienced by teachers, students, and parents, it is *assessment* (Toppo, 2007). More students now participate in more state standardized assessments, more often, than ever before. The state assessments are in addition to the classroom tests that teachers administer to monitor student progress or to assign midterm and end-of-course grades. Tests that reliably and validly measure student performance are central to the integrity of the overall accountability framework. The rationale behind frequent assessment is that education will improve if schools face consequences when students do not meet educational goals. Student assessment is thus the primary "agent of change" within accountability reforms.

One of the main issues when testing students with disabilities, including students who are deaf or hard of hearing, is the challenge students have in showing what they know on a standardized assessment (see Lollis & LaSasso, 2009, for a discussion of issues related to test item construction and format). Assessment practices for students with disabilities often include the use of accommodations to reduce barriers in accessing test content. Alternate assessments, or tests that do not use the standardized pencil-and-paper format, are also an emerging issue in accountability-based measurement. This chapter discusses issues of participation in assessment as they relate to what we know about academic achievement for students who are deaf or hard of hearing.

Assessment Accommodations

Educational assessment for students who are deaf or hard of hearing, particularly standardized tests, often includes the use of testing accommodations (Bolt & Thurlow, 2004; Tindal & Fuchs, 2000). The decision to use testing accommodations is documented on a student's Individualized Education Program (IEP) plan, required for students receiving services under IDEA and Section 504 of the Rehabilitation Act. Accommodations are meant to increase the number of students with disabilities who are able to meaningfully participate in standardized assessments (Phillips, 1994; the following section of this chapter is adapted from Cawthon, 2006, originally published in the *Journal of Deaf Studies and Deaf Education*).

Accommodations refers to a range of changes to test administration and test content that are designed to remove factors that penalize students because of their disability and not their knowledge of test material (Elliott & Braden, 2000; Elliott, Kratochwill, & McKevitt, 2001; Fuchs & Fuchs, 1999; Phillips, 2004; Shriner & DeStefano, 2003). For example, students with a visual impairment may receive a Braille version of the assessment, thus removing student inability to see the test as a barrier to their performance on the assessment. The *Standards for Educational and Psychological Testing* (American Educational Research Association, American Psychological Association, National Council on Measurement in Education, 1999) describes many test changes for students with disabilities under the general umbrella of accommodations. However, not all accommodations are considered equal or considered to have similar properties (Koretz & Barton, 2003; Pitoniak & Royer, 2001). Some accommodations, such as having a test item read aloud to a student when the test is of reading skills, may change the nature of the assessment. Accommodations, in this chapter, refer only to changes in test administration that do not also change the target skill of the assessment.

Assessment policies on a state and federal level articulate how accommodations are to be used within the context of accountability reforms. These policies are different in scope from accommodations guidelines used by postsecondary institutions for class placement or by companies that administer college entrance exams (The College Board, n.d.). The National Center for Education Outcomes publishes regular reports on state policies regarding assessments and accommodations for students with disabilities (e.g., Clapper, Morse, Lazarus, Thompson, & Thurlow, 2005; Lazarus, Thurlow, Lail, Eisenbraun, & Kato, 2006; Minnema, Thurlow, Anderson, & Stone, 2005; Wiley, Thurlow, & Klein, 2005). These reports indicate that state policies are more robust for students who only use one language than those who have English at school but another language at home. Furthermore, although students whose primary disability is hearing loss may come from homes where English is the family language, some of these students come from homes with other languages, including spoken or signed languages. There were few states with policies that explicitly outline accommodations for students who may fit in multiple language use groups.

All states have policies for how to include students with disabilities in standardized assessments (Clapper et al., 2005). As of 2006, some accommodations were "allowed without restriction," meaning that a test score with the accommodation was viewed to be as valid as an unaccommodated test score, and therefore, the score was included in overall aggregations of student scores. Large Print was designated as "allowed" in most states, as were Individual Administration, Sign Interpreting for directions, and Read Aloud directions. Policies for accommodations that change presentation of the test questions were less likely to be "allowed." Only three states allowed *questions* to be Read Aloud without restrictions, with the majority designating this accommodation as "allowed in certain circumstances" ($n = 31$) or "with implications for scoring" ($n = 13$). States were similarly cautious in policies to allow questions to be sign interpreted. The level of flexibility allowed in using test accommodations appears to be tied to whether they affect the test items, specifically, and not the setting or test directions.

In addition to policies for the above accommodations, Clapper et al. (2005) also collected data on response accommodations, or accommodations that change how the student gives answers to the test items. Most state policies allowed a range of response accommodations without restrictions, including a scribe, a computer, or writing entered directly in the test booklet instead of use of the bubble sheet. Fewer states allowed the student to use gestures such as pointing to the correct answer or responding with sign language to an interpreter, without restrictions and implications for scoring.

Using sign language for either the administration or participation in the assessment is thus an area of concern when seeking testing parity for students who are deaf or hard of hearing. Depending on the prevalence and type of accommodations used for students who are deaf or hard of hearing, these policy guidelines have an impact on how student scores are integrated into the overall accountability framework.

Because deafness is a low-incidence disability, there is very little information on the impact of testing accommodations with students who are deaf or hard of hearing (Johnson, 2004). Overall studies of testing accommodations for students with disabilities do not have sufficient numbers of students who are deaf or hard of hearing to report specific findings for this population. Luckner and Bowen (2006) have provided some early findings on what tests teachers use to evaluate student knowledge and skill in core content areas, but their findings are focused more on classroom assessments than on specific accommodation use during statewide standardized assessments. An early guide to accommodations for students who are deaf or hard of hearing suggested four options: (1) reduce the number of assessments, (2) provide an alternate assessment, (3) provide assistance in reading the test, and (4) provide extra time (Johnson, Benson, & Seton, 1997). Most of the available research for students who are deaf or hard of hearing looks at the effects of different communication modes as an accommodation in intelligence testing. For example, Sullivan and Schulte (1992) examined differences in test results when tests were administered by either the test administrator or an interpreter. Signed tests were signed in the child's mode of communication (e.g., American Sign Language or Signed Exact English) by the test administrator whereas the interpreted test was interpreted through a separate staff person. They found that there was little effect of administration on WISC-R intelligence test scores.

As part of my own efforts in this area, I have been working with teachers to develop an overall picture of accommodations used with students who are deaf or hard of hearing. The *National Survey of Accommodations and Assessments for Students Who Are Deaf or Hard of Hearing* (Cawthon & the Online Research Lab, 2006, 2007; Cawthon, Wurtz, & the Online Research Lab, 2008; Cawthon, Hersh, Kim, & the Online Research Lab, 2009) has, to date, collected information from the 2003–04, 2004–05, and 2005–06 statewide assessments. Cawthon and the Online Research Lab (2006, 2007) reported that students received a wide range of accommodations. Extended time and small groups were among the most popular accommodations, as was having the test directions interpreted. Accommodations that were used less frequently include having a student sign his or her response to a scribe or administering the test in a simplified English format (see Table 4.1).

Findings on accommodations use were similar for both mathematics and reading, with the exception of two accommodations: Read Aloud (test items are read to students) and Interpreted Test Items (test items are interpreted in Sign Language or the student's preferred sign system) (Cawthon & the Online Research Lab, 2006, 2007). Read Aloud and Interpreted Test Items are similar accommodations in that the student does not read the test item from a test booklet (the standardized format). Instead, the test item is presented in either spoken language (English in this case) or signed language (American Sign Language or other sign system) by the test administrator. Students who are deaf or hard of hearing were more likely to receive either

Table 4.1. Examples of Accommodations Used With Students Who Are Deaf or Hard of Hearing on Statewide Standardized Assessments for Accountability

Type of Accommodation	Description
Extended Time	Time and a half or double time is allowed on assessments that have time limits.
Small Groups or Individual Administration	Tests are given in a small group or to individual students, sometimes at a setting and time separate from the larger group.
Test Directions Interpreted	The test directions are provided either in American Sign Language or in the student's primary mode of communication.
Test Items Interpreted	The test items are provided either in American Sign Language or in the student's primary mode of communication.
Test Items Read Aloud	The test directions are read aloud to the student.
Student Signs Response	The student signs his or her responses (in American Sign Language or other sign system) to a scribe who then writes the answers down in a booklet or on a scantron sheet.
Simplified English	The test is written in a simpler form of English than in the standard administration.

accommodation for the mathematics portion of the test than for the reading portion. Although overall prevalence was lower than for Extended Time or Interpreter for Directions, the proportion of settings that used Read Aloud and Interpreted Responses as accommodations on standardized tests is quite high.

These are important findings in the context of the discussion of accommodations validity and state policies. There are concerns regarding the use of any accommodations that change the target skill in reading assessments from reading decoding to listening comprehension (Braden & Elliott, 2003; McKevitt & Elliott, 2003; Messick, 1995). Most state policies allow only Read Aloud or Sign Interpreted test items "in certain circumstances" (Clapper et al., 2005). Partly in reaction to questions regarding validity of tests taken with these accommodations, many states include restrictions on how scores can be included in their overall accountability frameworks. Test scores of students who are deaf or hard of hearing who use these accommodations may therefore be excluded from school and state reports of academic progress.

How a student's score is integrated into accountability decisions depends, in part, on the state policy in his or her state of residence. For most of the accommodations in Table 4.1, either students largely receive accommodations that allow for their score to be included or the accommodations are not prevalent enough to cause concern. However, Read Aloud Test Items and Interpreted Test Items show a more complex picture of policy and practice. For Read Aloud, only 3% of teachers using the accommodation work in states where it is allowed without implications. Approximately half (49%) work in states where it is allowed in certain circumstances, usually for tests that do not target reading skills. An additional 16% work in states that limit not only the tests during which Read Aloud can be used but also how the scores are aggregated. Student scores with Interpreted Test Items also have restrictions, but in contrast with Read Aloud, 40% of teachers who report using this accommodation live in states with implications for scoring.

In summary, assessment practices with students who are deaf or hard of hearing are complex, but concerns about the validity of test scores and inclusion in AYP accountability appears to be limited to Read Aloud and Interpreted Test Item accommodations. Accommodations for other students who are English Language Learners may pose similar concerns if test items are read to them in English or translated into their native language. Translated tests face potential validity issues, particularly if they are given orally in a nonstandardized format. When states consider translating tests for students who are not yet proficient in English, particularly for those tests that are not assessing reading skills, American Sign Language interpreters should be included in the discussion of alternate language formats.

Alternate Assessments

Although most students are expected to participate in standardized assessments, with or without accommodations, there are a few students for whom these assessments are inappropriate (Council for Exceptional Children, 2006; Quenemoen, Rigney, & Thurlow, 2002). For these students, alternate assessments may be used to gain an accurate evaluation of student proficiency in core content areas. However, alternate assessments are different from standardized assessments in several ways (Browder, Spooner, Algozzine, Ahlgrim-Delzell, Flowers, & Karvonen, 2003). Because of changes in how students are tested, alternate assessments change both the target skill and the access skill of the assessment. For example, deleting an item or changing an essay response into a multiple choice question are both examples of modifications that effectively change what is being measured by the assessment (Elliott, McKevitt, & Kettler, 2002). Alternate assessments are, in essence, comprehensive modifications to the standardized test format.

Most states have developed alternate assessments to allow students with the most severe cognitive disabilities to participate in accountability reforms. The format of these alternate assessments varies by state (Thompson, Johnstone, Thurlow, & Altman, 2005). For example, some states use a checklist of knowledge and skills that teachers fill out as part of the student's assessment evaluation. Other states allow teachers to compile a portfolio that is then scored using a standard rubric (Turner, Baldwin, Kleinert, & Kearns, 2000; Weiner, 2006). These examples are different from the standardized assessment because the student does not demonstrate her proficiency on a single test in a standardized format. Instead, the teacher (or teachers) provide documentation that is often based on extended periods of classroom activity. Alternate assessments are time intensive but allow students who cannot participate in a standardized test to demonstrate their knowledge and skills.

Questions of validity motivate both sides of the debate on how alternate assessments might allow students with disabilities to meaningfully participate in a state accountability framework (Flowers, Browder, Wakeman, & Karvonen, 2006; Towles, Garrett, Burdette, & Burdge, 2003). Quenemoen and Thurlow (2002) emphasize the importance of technically sound assessments and a clear process by which scores on alternate assessments are included in accountability decisions. If research shows that teacher effort is a major predictor of student proficiency scores on alternate assessments, then the test is evaluating what the teacher brings to the assessment process as much (or more) than student demonstration of knowledge and skill (Kampfer, Horvath, Kleinert, & Kearns, 2001). Technical quality issues such as validity in constructs measured and reliability in scoring are just as important for alternate assessments as they are for standardized tests (Kleinert & Kearns, 1999; Shepard, 1993). As some states move toward growth models of student proficiency, questions of scoring, especially over time, and of how these scores are included in discussions of school efficacy will only grow in their importance (Browder et al., 2003).

As part of the *National Survey of Accommodations and Assessments for Students Who Are Deaf or Hard of Hearing* (Cawthon & the Online Research Lab, 2006, 2007; Cawthon, Wurtz, and the Online Research Lab, 2008), participants also provided information about student participation in alternate assessments (Cawthon & the Online Research Lab, 2006, 2007). It is difficult to track the percentage of students who are Deaf or hard of hearing who participate in standardized versus alternate assessments on student performance report cards for schools. In this national sample of 7,646 students, the majority participated in standardized assessments *with* accommodations (70%). An additional 13% of students represented in this study participated in alternate assessments. The 10% who did not participate include students who were not enrolled for the entire school year or who were in grades that were not assessed in 2004–05.

Although fewer students participated in an alternate assessment than in a standardized assessment with accommodations, this method was still an important part of assessment practices at schools and programs that serve students who are deaf or hard of hearing. Data from this study represent alternate assessment practices for an estimated 900 students attending 71 schools and programs. The most prevalent forms of alternate assessment were Out-of-Level, Work Samples, and Portfolio approaches, each format being used by just under half of the responding participants. Close behind were curriculum-based assessments, selected by just over a third of these programs. Schools for the deaf were more likely than districtwide/school programs or mainstreamed settings to have students participate in alternate assessments. Figure 4.1 shows the percentage of teachers ($N = 339$) who indicated that at least one of their students who are deaf or hard of hearing used the alternate assessment format for the 2004–05 statewide assessments.

There are two main validity concerns with the forms of alternate assessment most often used with students who are deaf or hard of hearing. The first relates to Out-of-Level testing. Out-of-Level testing refers to having students take a test at a different (usually lower) level from their same-aged peers (Van Getson, Minnema, & Thurlow, 2004). However, because Out-of-Level testing was allowed in only 12 states in this assessment year (Clapper et al., 2005), and mostly with restrictions, the prevalence of this format (see Figure 4.1) is higher than expected. Because most states use caution when interpreting scores of tests that use Out-of-Level forms of an assessment, students who use this format may not be equally represented in NCLB accountability frame-

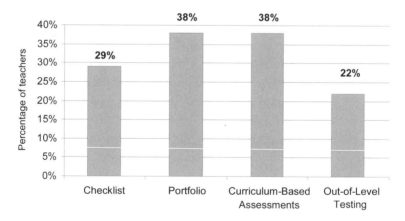

Figure 4.1. Percentage of teachers who had at least one student use alternate assessment format for 2004–05 statewide assessments. From Alternate Assessment Use With Students Who Are Deaf or Hard of Hearing: An Exploratory Mixed Methods Analysis of Predictors of Portfolio, Checklists, and Out-of-Level Testing Formats by S. Cawthon, K. Wurtz, & the Online Research Lab, 2008, *Journal of Deaf Studies and Deaf Education, 14,* 155–77.

works. This concern is similar to those for Read Aloud and Signed Question-Response accommodations found for standardized assessments.

The second validity concern focuses on student-constructed alternate assessments such as those used by many of the students in this study. Work Samples, Portfolio, and Curriculum-Based approaches are all rooted in the students' daily activities. If the curriculum and classroom instruction are aligned to state standards, then it is likely that alternate assessments using work samples and other artifacts also meet required standards (Flowers et al., 2006). However, classroom instruction and student activities that are not closely aligned to state standards may result in alternate assessments that cannot demonstrate student proficiency on required elements. This issue is not specific to students who are deaf or hard of hearing but to all students who participate in alternate assessments (Kleinert & Kearns, 1999; Ralabate, 2006). Yet because of the prevalence of alternate assessment use for students who are deaf or hard of hearing, the findings from the *National Survey* emphasize the importance of quality alternate assessment development and integration into NCLB accountability frameworks (Browder et al., 2003).

Recommendations for Action

There is much work to be done in the area of assessment for students who are deaf or hard of hearing. Whereas the content area recommendations focused mainly on what is measured, these assessment recommendations address the methods behind testing, or how student knowledge is measured. As with the previous recommendations on content area standards, I break down the assessment recommendations into three categories: (a) policy, (b) research, and (c) practice.

There are several policy recommendations related to the assessment process. The first recommendation is for states to have consistent accommodations policies. State policies for accommodations currently vary widely. Although it is challenging for states to standardize the content of their tests or the cut scores for proficiency, the accommodations policies could be standardized without jeopardizing individual state's rights over educational content. Most urgently, a national panel on accommodations use for students who are deaf or hard of hearing is essential to providing guidelines to states on how to treat test scores of students who use an interpreter for test items, either orally or through signed communication, or who take a test in simplified English.

A second assessment policy area is eligibility for alternate assessments. Currently, only those students with the most severe disabilities are eligible to take an alternate assessment and have their score count toward accountability tallies. Many students who are deaf or hard of hearing have additional disabilities, and even if none of them are severe, the combination of those disabilities makes participation in a standardized test format most difficult. If these students take the alternate assessment but are beyond the "cap" of students whose scores are eligible, then the assessment process is rendered meaningless within accountability reforms. My recommendation is to raise the cap on the percentage of students eligible to use the alternate assessment, or remove the cap all together. The cap itself is artificial when applied to individual students in a school setting. This artificiality is particularly true for schools or districts that serve more than the average number of students with disabilities; the cap is derived from an overall measure of the prevalence of students with severe disabilities that often does not apply to schools with specific programs, including those for students who are deaf or hard of hearing.

Research recommendations for this section arise mainly in the areas of measurement. The first is a need for controlled, empirical study of the effects of accommodations on test scores for students who are deaf or hard of hearing. This kind of study is particularly important because students who are deaf or hard of hearing use accommodations that are not largely used by other students. Accommodations that include interpreted test items or simplified English may be parallel to those used by English Language Learning students, but the research needs to address specifically the effects of these accommodations for students who are deaf or hard of hearing. There are small efforts currently under way (Cawthon, Winton, Garberoglio, & Gobble, in press); a coordinated effort will only strengthen the conclusions that can be drawn from these results.

A second area of research is the development and evaluation of growth models that are tailored to the needs of students who are deaf or hard of hearing. A major issue in the implementation of NCLB has been the tension between assessment standardization and individualized decision making about assessment practices for students with disabilities (Koretz & Barton, 2003). For example, IEP recommendations are based on individual student characteristics, yet standardized, one-size-fits-all testing is the primary mechanism for accountability reforms. The kind of research project needed requires the input of parents, teachers, students, researchers, psychometricians, and policymakers. The project could unfold in the following sequence: (a) identify learning goals for students who are deaf or hard of hearing; (b) include those goals not only in state content standards but also in areas that are important specifically for students who are deaf or hard of hearing; (c) develop reliable methods to measure them; and (d) create proficiency targets that take into consideration the student's individual characteristics, available resources, and personal goals. In a sense, this idea expands on the IEP development process used for individual students and creates a format for it to be implemented statewide for students who are deaf or hard of hearing. A related policy recommendation is to use multiple sources when evaluating student progress; the research in this area can complement the policy change by providing a robust measure that is still flexible enough for students who are deaf or hard of hearing.

A third area of needed research is in how to establish and interpret alternate assessment scores. Future research will play an important role in helping to form responses to questions in the field and in policy regarding alternate assessments and proficiency scores. One concern about alternate assessments relates to the subjectivity of teachers or other educational professionals who evaluate student performance. The benefit of standardized assessments is that all students are evaluated on the same task, with little interpretation of whether the skill has been demonstrated (though there is a great deal of discussion about the ability of the test to measure the skill, a related validity issue). Alternate assessments also require rigorous standards for evaluating and scoring student performance of knowledge and skill. Researchers can contribute to developing our knowledge of how rubrics or other tools for quantifying student progress can help make alternate assessment scores a viable component of an overall accountability system. Understanding what it means not only to be proficient but also to make progress in developing conceptual knowledge is one way that alternate assessments can make a valuable contribution to our assessment repertoire. Taken as a process, these kinds of studies can help connect the multiple factors that contribute to the process and implications of assessment practices for students who are deaf or hard of hearing.

Change in practice is perhaps the most challenging area in which to make recommendations due to the constraints posed by the current accountability and testing policy environment. One recommendation stems from the findings about the effects of test practice on resultant scores. Students who have had practice taking tests in the same format as those they take on the assessment day do better than those who may have the same knowledge base, but are unfamiliar with the test layout and structure (Kornhaber & Orfield, 2001). Students who are deaf or hard of hearing who may receive instruction in American Sign Language but take the test in written English must process a kind of "code-switching" between languages that is even more extreme than the processing required for students who make the transition from classroom dialogue to the language of a standardized test. Teachers and administrators might think about how to develop these needed test-taking skills as part of the preparation for statewide large-scale assessments.

A second practice recommendation is for states to provide lists of key vocabulary words on the assessment to teachers with students who use American Sign Language or other signed communication. This information would help teachers to prepare students by using the signs that they are familiar with to make the connections with test vocabulary. The research on glossary and dictionary use as an accommodation during assessment is mixed (Kieffer, Lesaux, Rivera, & Francis, 2009), indicating that prior preparation with key vocabulary words may be more effective than using a reference guide on the test day itself.

The final practice recommendation is to include interpreters in any discussion of assessment for students who are deaf or hard of hearing. Some states allow provisions for the same person who provides accommodations for classroom instruction to provide accommodations during standardized assessment. Inclusion of interpreters in discussions about alternate assessment is equally critical to ensure that students have access to the test content. Input from interpreters is particularly important for students in regular education settings who rely on an interpreter to have access to classroom content. Interpreters need adequate time to review the test, clarify vocabulary words, strategize on ways to prevent threats to validity resulting from how a question is signed, and participate in discussion on what the student's needs might be as far as frequent breaks or extended time. If the student is going to sign responses, there should be clarification as to whether the interpreter is recording those answers "verbatim" or translating back into English-structured sentences. States or districts may want to formalize the training for their state assessments by including workshops for interpreters or test administrators who are using such accommodations.

Conclusion

"In reading the law [NCLB] and its associated regulations, it is not always clear where the challenges leave off and the opportunities begin" (Kingsbury, Olson, Cronin, Hauser, & Houser, 2004, p. 1). Accountability assessment, in its conceptual form, is a straightforward process. Schools hire teachers, teachers provide instruction based on state standards, students learn content in core academic areas, and students demonstrate their proficiency in those areas on state assessments. In reality, this process is anything but simple, particularly for students who are deaf or hard of hearing. For example, it is not clear that the content standards for literacy development, as they are outlined in state standards and measured by state assessments, allow enough flexibility for diverse approaches to literacy instruction used by teachers of students who are deaf or hard of hearing. Because the *match* between standards, pedagogy, student learning, and assessment is left out of the discussion of evaluating school effectiveness, data provided by accountability give very little information about how to raise student achievement. Accountability's components, while logical when taken individually, do not lead to a holistically appropriate sequence for students with disabilities or those from linguistically diverse backgrounds.

Assessment strategies will continue to play a critical role in how students participate in accountability and how educational structures (schools, districts, and states) are evaluated. Historically low rates of proficiency and gains in achievement indicate that students with hearing loss may not fare well on state standardized assessments. Alternate assessment strategies appear to give more positive evaluation of student skills, but we do not yet have a way to look at the overall impact of alternate assessments on proficiency scores for students who are deaf or hard of hearing. In other words, it is not clear whether alternate assessments inflate proficiency ratings or whether they provide information that is not available on a standardized assessment (even with accommodations). While "growth" or "value-added" models may provide a more accurate picture of the contribution of a single year's instruction to student knowledge, using these scores in an accountability framework may prove to be more complicated for students with disabilities than for those without.

5

Accountability and Schools

Schools are the "units of accountability" within the structure of accountability reform. In other words, test score reports and evaluation of success or failure begins primarily at the school level, not at the teacher or student level. Although some states have teacher-centered accountability through merit pay programs based on student test scores, schools are the primary focus when reporting student progress on state assessments. The many educational structures that serve students who are deaf or hard of hearing experience accountability in different ways. On the whole, settings that stand alone and are considered separate from other structures, for example, schools that serve special populations (e.g., schools for the deaf) receive more attention in accountability reforms than specialized programs that are combined or share resources with regular education. Test scores for students who are deaf or hard of hearing at district programs or regular education settings are combined with those for larger groups of students such as students with disabilities. Accountability reforms are thus less salient for settings that have more integration with peers than for schools for the deaf. Schools for the deaf therefore serve as a focal point for how current accountability reform affects educational structures that serve students who are deaf or hard of hearing.

Accountability as Sanctions

Accountability reform, if implemented in an accurate and fair manner, has the potential to reward those schools that provide quality education to students and to provide consequences for those that do not. As outlined in Chapter 2, in the current version of accountability legislation (NCLB), the focus is on the consequences, or the sanctions, for not meeting annual performance benchmarks. A reward for meeting these benchmarks is primarily the *absence* of sanctions, not tangible gain in resources or local control. NCLB therefore relies on the "sticks" more than the "carrots" that may be used in other versions of accountability reform (Abernathy, 2007). Although future reauthorizations may emphasize a different mix of incentives, any new models will be layered on the accountability framework currently in place. The next section of this chapter looks at the details of these sanctions in greater detail.

One thing to note about the current accountability approach is the progressive nature of sanctions. NCLB designations for Title I schools that do not meet AYP guidelines get increasingly serious the longer those schools appear on the "in need of improvement" list (20 U.S.C. Section 6316(b)). As outlined in Chapter 3, Title I schools are those that receive federal funding to increase educational opportunity for students from low-income backgrounds. Even if individual schools do not serve large numbers of students from low-income backgrounds, almost all districts participate in the Title I program and receive federal funds. (Depending on the individual state policy, non-Title I schools may receive a state report card and face sanctions.)

A list of the AYP sanctions is given in Table 5.1. In Year 1 of not meeting AYP, schools are labeled "in need of improvement." There are no sanctions in the first year; schools are essentially given a warning before tangible consequences occur. After two consecutive years of failing to meet AYP, parents of Title I children in the school are given the option of transferring their children to another school in the district. This option is referred to as "public school choice," and the district is responsible for transportation to the new school until the original school has met AYP goals for two consecutive years (discussed further in Chapter 7). In Year 3, the school must provide supplemental services such as tutoring and after-school programs to Title I students who remain at the school. Year 4 of not meeting AYP benchmarks brings potential changes in staff, curriculum, and reorganization of the management

Table 5.1. NCLB Consequences

Year "In Need of Improvement"	Consequence
Year 1	Formal warning
Year 2	NCLB public school choice
Year 3	Supplemental services
Year 4	Initial changes to staff, curriculum, or structure
Year 5	State reconstitution of school, staff restructuring, or management change to charter school

structure. Finally, Year 5 of not meeting AYP benchmarks results in making a large-scale change in teaching staff, reopening the school as a charter school site, or establishing state management of the school. For schools for the deaf that are already run by the state, restructuring or charter options are more likely than continuing with the same school administration.

One important consideration in understanding accountability-based reform is the stringency of its criteria. In other words, are the consequences directed at a few underperforming participants or are they to be applied to all participants? This question is relevant on the student level, teacher level, school level, or district level. For example, if severe consequences are meant only for those on the lowest end of the performance scale, reflected, say, in the number of Fs a teacher might give in a class, then the expectation is that most participants can achieve the stated goals (i.e., pass the class). In contrast, if there are benchmarks that must be met, regardless of previous performance or demonstration that participants have the capacity to meet these goals, then it is possible that all or most will fail the test. This second scenario would be similar to an achievement test where only a few students are expected to pass, thus selecting only the exemplary performers in the group. This approach might be used when the goal is to select only the very best candidates for a highly selective position or program such as an astronaut or Olympic athlete. The remaining set would be expected to fail, or be "weeded out," in this scenario.

In truth, most assessments in education follow the first model where most participants are expected to meet at least adequate levels of performance.

Teachers in classes where most students fail would not have a long career in education. In other words, we do not, in general, set up students or teachers or schools with the expectation that only a few will succeed. Whether this approach is adopted because we expect reasonable efforts to be rewarded, or at least not punished, is unclear. In a sense, there is a "social promotion" model for schools wherein, even if their students do not meet grade-level expectations, the schools are still passed along as meeting minimum requirements.

NCLB does not follow this approach. Instead, the form of accountability in this legislation sets the bar very high—all students to meet proficiency by 2014—even though schools have never produced student performance at this level at any point in history (Abernathy, 2007). State benchmarks for higher achievement, even those with multi-year targets, will soon rise to meet the 100% proficiency goals. Early predictions of the impact of NCLB estimated that as many as 80% of schools would come under corrective measures by the end of the NCLB time frame (Olson, 2002). As of the 2007–08 school year, the percentage of schools that did not make AYP ranged from 7% in Wisconsin and Oklahoma to 87% in South Carolina. Furthermore, an additional seven states had 60% or more of their schools listed as not meeting AYP (Olson, 2005b). In all but eight states, the percentages of schools not making AYP represented an increase over the 2006–07 school year. As time moves toward 2014, it is likely that the list of schools in each state that have not made AYP will continue to grow.

Will NCLB sanctions for schools in Years 4 and 5 of "in need of improvement" result in a large-scale overhaul of public schools (Lee, 2004)? The possibility of overhaul on this scale remains to be seen. Early predictions did not take into account a number of changes in how states interpret the law, for example, the use of large minimum group sizes, the practice of averaging data over more than one assessment year, changes in proficiency standards, the use of confidence intervals, and safe harbor provisions (Lee, 2004). The wide range of results for states with schools that did not meet AYP reflects the great diversity in how standards and accountability measures are implemented from state to state. Furthermore, even in a state with a high percentage of schools that have not met AYP, far fewer schools are on the list of schools identified as in need of improvement. For example, in Florida, 76% of schools did not meet AYP in 2007–08, but only 28% are on the list for sanctions. This discrepancy may occur because not all schools are Title

I schools and/or because schools need to fail to meet AYP for more than 1 year to face sanctions. In the future, Congress may reauthorize NCLB with changes to the scope of consequences and provide a positive incentive for greater identification of struggling schools. Even with a modest improvement in student achievement, the true level of consequences for schools will vary by state definitions of proficiency, data reporting policies, and later adjustments to federal law.

One strong advantage of accountability is the transparency it brings to how states measure and report student achievement (Thompson & Thurlow, 2003; Thurlow & Wiley, 2004). As part of compliance with NCLB, states submitted *Consolidated State Application Accountability Workbooks* to the U.S. Department of Education (DOE) in January, 2003. These workbooks followed a common template, but vary greatly in how they are completed from state to state. These plans were then reviewed by the DOE and revised over the course of the first few years of their implementation. These plans include comprehensive articulation of how the state will aggregate and report data for all students. The accountability workbooks discuss how the accountability system includes all schools and districts, uses content standards to document proficiency, and clearly documents how accountability decisions will be made. As part of these plans, states documented how data for students attending *special* schools would be incorporated into the overall assessment and accountability framework. States responded to a series of Principles of NCLB, including Principle 1.1: *Accountability system includes all schools and districts in the state.* Section 1.1 of the Accountability Workbook asks how

[t]he State Accountability System produces AYP decisions for all public schools, includ.ing public schools with variant grade configurations (e.g., K–12), *public schools that serve special populations (e.g., alternative public schools, juvenile institutions, state public schools for the blind)* and public charter schools. It also holds accountable public schools with no grades assessed (e.g., K–2). (U.S. Department of Education, 2003, Section 1.1, emphasis added)

The current text for Principle 1.1 in the New Mexico's *Consolidated State Application Accountability Workbook* serves as a specific example:

All 808 public schools in New Mexico receive public funds. Each public school in New Mexico is assigned a separate identification code. Of these schools, 586 public schools from 89 school districts receive Title I funds. Each of the 89 school districts has a separate district identification code. Alternative schools (state supported residential schools, including the School for the Visually Impaired, New Mexico School for the Deaf, Mimbres School-Children's Psychiatric Center and the Juvenile Detention Facilities) have separate district codes. Charter schools have the same district code from the district in which they are located and a separate school code. (New Mexico State Department of Education, 2008)

This aspect of the accountability plan is useful when looking for information about how each state will measure student performance at schools for the deaf. It is these guidelines that lay the groundwork for how states report student performance and evaluate school effectiveness.

Student proficiency rates, along with other indicators such as attendance and high school graduation rates, form the core of the reports of AYP for each school and district. The school report cards lay out the assessment and additional factors used to evaluate school progress under NCLB. For each category, schools must meet the state benchmarks to make AYP. Thus, if a school does not meet the state benchmarks in *even one cell* in the table, the school is listed as "in need of improvement." This level of severity is akin to a person failing an exam whether he or she misses one problem or all of the problems on a test. These guidelines certainly present tight benchmarks that schools and districts must meet to demonstrate success in raising student proficiency for all students in core content areas. The effects of NCLB will be shown, in part, by changes in the school profiles represented on AYP report cards.

Students With Disabilities

Schools are diverse settings, often serving students across a variety of ethnic, socioeconomic, and cultural backgrounds. Schools also have students with a range of moderating factors in their level of achievement, including students with disabilities that affect how they access grade-level curricula. By requiring schools to report the performance of major student subgroups, NCLB formalizes and strengthens previous guidelines for including students with disabilities in high-stakes assessment. Previous accountability measures allowed states to look at overall progress, masking the lack of progress of some students with calculations of average performance of all students. To maintain accountability for *all* students, NCLB legislation requires states to disaggregate school performance data by the following groups:

- Primary ethnic groups (e.g., Caucasian, African American, Hispanic, Asian)
- English Language Learners
- Low-income students
- Students with disabilities

For the purpose of NCLB accountability legislation, students who are deaf or hard of hearing fall under the students with disabilities group. Although this designation may not be appropriate for all students with hearing loss, and is protested by some in the deaf community (Lane, 1999), it is here where we find information more specific to students who are deaf or hard of hearing. On most reports cards for schools for the deaf, the entire enrollment is reported under the students with disabilities category.

When NCLB was first passed, there was a great deal of concern that schools and districts would be penalized for test scores of students with disabilities. Students with disabilities have a larger achievement gap to overcome, but the accountability system in place gives them less time to make the same rate of progress as their peers (Edwards, 2004). In other words, students with disabilities have to meet the same goal (100% proficiency), at the same end point (2014), but generally start from further behind. Because students with disabilities typically have slower rates of improvement in each grade, this expectation is a double whammy for both students and teachers. The initial (and continuing) fear was that schools would blame the teachers of students with disabilities for being the only subgroup that did not meet achievement benchmarks, thus making the whole school ineligible for AYP. Although accountability for all students is a laudable goal, having it turn into a blame game within a school is anything but constructive.

The impact of subgroups on AYP status depends, in part, on the number of subgroups within the school. When a school serves students with a variety of ethnic backgrounds, students with a range of English language proficiency, and students who are from low-income families, the school has a higher number of subgroup categories that it must show on its AYP report card. In contrast with schools with a homogenous student body, a diverse school has to meet more criteria to reach AYP. Novak and Fuller (2003) make the case that this policy unfairly punishes schools in low-income and urban areas. Because students who are English Language Learners are also more likely to be of different ethnic backgrounds and from low-income families, their scores are counted multiple times within a single report card. Schools with a greater number of subgroups (up to six in this analysis) were far less likely to make AYP than those with only one or two student subgroups. For example, within the group of schools with at least 75% of students from low-income families, 16% of schools with six subgroups passed whereas 53% of schools with one subgroup made AYP. *Even when academic achievement of students is held constant*, a large number of subgroups reduces the likelihood of the school making AYP.

"Minimum group size" is an emerging issue that has a significant impact on how students with disabilities (and other subgroups) are included in AYP decisions. States determine the minimum number of students that need to be within each group before their scores are reported and used in AYP calculations (Erpenbach, Forte-Fast, & Potts, 2003). The purpose of establishing a minimum group size is to limit the potential loss of anonymity of student scores, guaranteed under the Family Educational Rights and Privacy Act (20 U.S.C. Sec. 1232g; 34 CFR Part 99). However, there are cases where the minimum group number is set so high ($n = 50$, for example) that it limits disaggregations of subgroups, including students with disabilities, to only very large schools.

The impact of minimum group size policies depends on each state's accountability plan and the number of students in that group at a given school (Simpson, Gong, & Marion, 2006). Across the country, only a small percentage of schools have enough students with disabilities to have a reportable subgroup on AYP report cards. For example, in California, only 8% of schools had enough students with disabilities to meet the minimum group size requirement for 2004–05 assessment scores (Olson, 2005a). As states continue to revise their minimum group sizes, or to include a minimum percentage of the student enrollment in these cutoffs, fewer schools will have their AYP based on subgroup performance. So while the format of AYP report cards had some potential for including students with disabilities in accountability decisions, the high minimum group sizes set by states preclude most schools from being "accountable" for their student achievement (Simpson et al. 2006). Schools with numbers of students with disabilities smaller than the minimum group size include the scores for students with disabilities with those of the overall student enrollment. This approach has the potential effect of "masking" or burying what may be lower scores for students with disabilities within the overall higher average score of the entire student body.

What do accountability mechanisms mean for students who are deaf or hard of hearing? Educational setting is a significant factor in how high-stakes decisions affect this target population because students who are deaf or hard of hearing are taught in both stand-alone and mainstreamed classrooms. The next section discusses how AYP affects students in regular education settings, district programs, and schools for the deaf.

Regular education settings are the least (directly) affected by the consequences of accountability for students who are deaf or hard of hearing. The most significant issues for students in mainstreamed settings are those that face students with disabilities as a whole: how accommodations affect the inclusion of test scores, large minimum group sizes for AYP subgroup analysis, and the use of confidence intervals in AYP calculations (Cawthon, 2007). Regular education schools *are* accountable for students with disabilities. However, there is little identifiable information, if any, for students who are deaf or hard of hearing as a group within regular education schools.

As discussed in Chapter 2, the IDEA calculations to determine the population of students who are deaf or hard of hearing in regular education schools likely underestimate the true population. A student would be counted toward the students with disabilities group as a student who is deaf or hard of hearing only if his or her hearing loss is listed as the *primary* disability. Students who are deaf or hard of hearing with multiple disabilities, of which hearing loss is secondary, may also be in the students with disabilities group, but not under the subgroup of students who are deaf or hard of hearing. Because of the way the report cards are structured, with reports of the percentage of students within a category meeting proficiency, it is also possible to double-count students across multiple categories. In fact, the proficiency rates of most students who are English Language Learners or who have a disability will be reported first by their primary ethnic group and then by their English Language Learner or disability status. Students within multiple categories may therefore count for or against a school's overall proficiency rates more than once. Recall that a school fails to meet AYP if even one category of student does not meet the proficiency rate benchmark (e.g., only 50% of students reach proficiency). A school for the deaf where all students fall within at least two categories (i.e., ethnicity and disability) would therefore have a greater number of categories of students that need to demonstrate proficiency for the school to make AYP.

Students who are deaf or hard of hearing are low-incidence not only in the overall student population but also within the students with disabilities group. Outside of schools for the deaf, students who are deaf or hard of hearing make up only a very small proportion of the overall students with disabilities population, the closest level of aggregation on school report cards. The percentage of students with a "hearing impairment" who were enrolled in a separate (nonresidential) school ranged from 0% to 34% across the 50 states, the District of Columbia, and the Bureau of Indian Education schools, with an overall average of nearly 8% (U.S. Office of Special Education Programs, 2007). The percentage of students with a hearing impairment who spent greater than 80% of their time inside regular education classrooms, in contrast, ranged from 21% (Hawaii) to 69% (Minnesota), with an overall average of 52%.

Given this variety of placements in regular education settings, the relative proportion of students who are deaf or hard of hearing among students with disabilities will vary by school. On the one hand, if a mainstreamed school has only a small population of students with other disabilities, then AYP reports for mainstreamed schools might change based on the progress made by one or two students who are deaf or hard of hearing attending that school. On the other hand, a large population of students with disabilities at a school means that the scores of students who are deaf or hard of hearing have relatively little weight in the overall aggregation of student performance. The attention paid to students who are deaf or hard of hearing may therefore be related to the overall makeup of the student body.

Another issue that arises in regular education settings is the idea of providing extra attention to the "bubble kids." The term *bubble kid* refers to students who may be close, but not quite at, state cutoff points for proficiency. Some schools will use mid-term assessments to identify those students who may be on the "bubble" toward counting as proficient for the statewide assessments later in the year. These students then receive supplementary instruction and test-taking preparation in an effort to push them over the bubble. Students who are very far behind the proficiency cutoff score are not a part of the extra push because it is unlikely that their scores could be raised enough to change the accountability report card outcomes. One teacher who was interviewed by Neal and Schanzenbach (2007) shared, "We were told to cross off the kids who would never pass. We were told to cross off the kids who, if we handed them the test tomorrow, they would pass. And then the kids who were left over, those were the kids we were supposed to focus on" (p. 1).

Are students who are deaf or hard of hearing bubble kids? Overall estimates of student proficiency make it very difficult to know whether students who are deaf or hard of hearing might be targeted as being "on the bubble." However, it is clear from the results presented in Chapter 4 that students who are deaf or hard of hearing, as a group, are on the lower end of the distribution of achievement scores on statewide, standardized assessments. Previous research indicates that students who are on the edges of academic success receive more attention *if they are in smaller school schools than in larger ones* (Cullen & Reback, 2006). Because AYP report cards use percentage of student populations to determine ratings, smaller schools have more to gain by a single student's attainment of "proficiency." In small schools, each additional student represents a greater percentage of the student body than in larger ones. The implication is that regular education schools, where students who are deaf or hard of hearing generally represent a smaller proportion of the overall population, would be less likely to consider students who are deaf or hard of hearing as bubble kids worthy of intensive instruction. If, as trends have indicated, students below the bubble do not receive the extra push to succeed on state tests, it is possible that students who are deaf or hard of hearing will be left even further behind their peers. When schools need to think about allocating resources toward improving results on accountability report cards, then students who need even further assistance, for example, students who are deaf or hard of hearing—especially those who are learning English at the same time as they are learning to read—may wind up shortchanged (Viadero, 2007).

Another setting where students are taught is district programs that serve students from schools in the region. Districts are accountable for student proficiency, but district AYP report cards offer no information about the effectiveness of *programs* for special populations, specifically. District programs for students who are deaf or hard of hearing are not like stand-alone schools for the deaf because they do not receive a single report card that holds the program accountable for student achievement (Schemo, 2004). Instead, student scores are sent back to the referring, or sending school, dispersing the student scores across the district. If students are not meeting proficiency, it is possible that the sending school may exert some pressure on the district program to change instructional strategies for students who are deaf or hard of hearing to raise their own school report card ratings.

District programs may affect *district* AYP designations to the extent that students in their programs make up a large proportion of the students with disabilities within the district. (Districts also receive report cards.) For example, depending on the number of other students scoring below proficiency, scores from students who are deaf or hard of hearing may alter whether the district meets state proficiency benchmarks. There are also similar concerns about the inclusion of student test scores that were obtained using accommodations such as test items read aloud or interpreted. (Accommodations for students who are deaf or hard of hearing are discussed in depth in Chapter 4.) Although students with IEPs are entitled to assessment accommodations, there are limits as to which accommodations are allowed on the high-stakes standardized assessment used for accountability. Policies tend to be strict with regard to accommodations that change the presentation of the test item such as those often used with students who are deaf or hard of hearing (Cawthon, 2007; Cawthon & the Online Research Lab, 2006, 2007). District programs that administer many assessments with the restricted accommodations may affect the number of reportable test scores for the district as a whole.

Finally, concerns about the use number of students using alternate or modified achievement standards are most salient for districts with large programs for students with disabilities. States have the option of developing alternate and modified achievement standards for students with disabilities who cannot be assessed at grade level. *Alternate* standards were part of the original NCLB guidelines and are meant for students who are significantly cognitively delayed. Students who are deaf or hard of hearing are largely not eligible for alternate standards. Yet for students who are deaf or hard of hearing, along with students with moderate disabilities who have some exposure to grade-level content but are not performing on grade level, there were no meaningful assessment options. Final NCLB regulations released in April 2007 included the new category of *modified* achievement standards to address this assessment gap. A modified achievement standard is based on the same content as the regular standards and is still challenging for eligible students, but is less difficult than grade-level achievement standards. A modified achievement standard is also more rigorous than the alternate achievement standard. The modified standards are designed for students with delays due to their disability despite appropriate instruction. IEP teams track student progress and justify the choice of using modified achievement standards if students are unlikely to reach grade-level performance within the year's time frame. Students who are deaf or hard of hearing may be eligible if a state implements the modified achievement standard process.

These additional assessment options are meant to provide flexibility for districts in how they assess students with disabilities. *There are, however, limits (i.e., caps) on how many students can participate in these special testing programs.* There is a 1% cap on students who use the alternate achievement standard and, more relevant to this conversation, a 2% cap on the number of students in any one grade who can use a modified assessment (U.S. Department of Education, 2007b). Thus, if a state provides an assessment based on modified standards for students in a single grade, the 2% calculation is based on the total number of students in that one grade. For example, if a school has 50 students in third grade, then a maximum of one student can take the assessment based on the modified standards and have the scores count for proficiency ratings. There are provisions for up to one additional percentage point (in this case, half of a student!) if the school has not used the alternate achievement standard quota. Scores for tests taken above these quotas cannot be counted as proficient on the school or district report card. When programs for students who are deaf or hard of hearing use modified achievement standards during NCLB assessment, it impacts the overall count of students who fit into the cap. Therefore, as with accountability for students in mainstreamed settings, accountability for district programs for deaf or hard of hearing students is related to the makeup of AYP reports for students with disabilities as a whole.

In contrast with mainstreamed settings and regional programs, schools for the deaf are the only type of educational setting that might receive its own report cards and, specifically, AYP designation for test scores of students who are deaf or hard of hearing. Whether a school for the deaf itself is accountable for student test scores depends on the state policy for special education schools. States can decide whether a school for the deaf will receive its own report card or whether student scores will be sent back to the sending or re-ferring district. In the accountability plan, states discuss how they are going to include all students in their assessment and data reporting frameworks, including those in special schools such as schools for the deaf.

As of 2006, there were 45 states (including the District of Columbia) with publicly funded schools for the deaf. In just under two-thirds of the states, schools for the deaf receive their own school report card and AYP status (Cawthon, 2004, 2008). About a third of these states report student data at either the sending or referring school or the district. Two states exempt schools for the deaf from state testing, and one state, Tennessee, aggregates data for students at schools for the deaf to the state level for accountability purposes.

Schools for the deaf that receive their own report card should also receive their own AYP designation. In 2004, 11 schools had a school report card with an AYP designation, and 16 schools had a report card without an AYP desig-nation (Cawthon, 2004). The number of schools with a report card doubled one year later to 23 schools (Cawthon, 2007). Approximately 25% of schools for the deaf reporting data meet AYP guidelines (Cawthon, 2004, 2008). However, there is still a great deal of missing information regarding student proficiency and AYP status for schools for the deaf. As of 2008, 8 states that have a school for the deaf *and* a policy for reporting data at the school level had neither a report card nor AYP designation for their school for the deaf (Cawthon, under review). This discrepancy may be occurring because scores are reported internally and not on public Web sites or because states have not been consistent in their application of Principle 1.1 from the accountability workbooks. Because looking at schools for the deaf that have report cards is the only direct way to see the impact of NCLB on educational structures that serve students who are deaf or hard of hearing, increasing the number of reporting mechanisms available will be an important part of how we track the implementation of accountability reform.

Technical issues that affect AYP calculations for small schools are salient in the discussion of report cards for schools for the deaf. Schools that serve only a small population face special challenges in NCLB calculations on AYP report cards (Erpenbach et al., 2003). Enrollments at state schools for the deaf range from just under 40 students (Montana School for the Deaf and Blind) to over 500 students (Florida School for the Deaf and Blind) (Moores,

2008a). These enrollments include K–12 and often combine not only the population of students who are deaf and blind but also students served by outreach programs. AYP report cards can disaggregate student scores by campus (e.g., deaf vs. blind or elementary vs. high school), tested subject (e.g., math, reading, science), each assessment grade (e.g., Grade 3, Grade 4, etc.), and student group (e.g., by ethnicity), resulting in far smaller numbers of students for each AYP criterion. It is the number of students per cell (or disaggregated amount) that must meet the minimum group size for reporting.

Schools for the deaf with an AYP report card in a state with a very low minimum group size (e.g., Maryland, with a minimum of $n = 5$) are more likely to report individual grade proficiency rates than schools in a state with a high minimum group size (as with California, $n = 100$, though this number varies by size of school and percentage of school population in subgroup). A school will automatically meet AYP designations if there are not enough students to meet the minimum n for data reporting. Although many schools for the deaf enroll more than the minimum for data reporting, often there are not enough students in the assessed grade (e.g., Grade 8 or Grade 10) to meet these requirements. Of the 16 states with report cards for their schools for the deaf, five did not report data because there was an insufficient sample of student scores for the assessed grade (Cawthon, in press). In Arizona, Florida, Hawaii, Rhode Island, and Washington, the minimum n was too high for school for the deaf to report student proficiency by grade. These findings confirm research that suggests that a rise in minimum n results in exclusion of students with disabilities from the accountability framework (Simpson et al., 2006).

A second challenge for AYP report cards at schools for the deaf is in how small student populations interact with the use of confidence intervals. Confidence intervals are a range of values (in this case, the percentage of students who meet proficiency) that are considered to "meet" AYP benchmarks. This approach contrasts with having a single percentage point (i.e., 95%) as a cutoff for proficiency. Using confidence intervals can help account for some of the statistical error involved in measuring group performance on tests. However, when combined with small group sizes, confidence intervals can result in misleading interpretations of student scores. The smaller the group size, the larger the range of scores that statistically meet the criteria for passing the benchmark target. Large confidence intervals (or those with high confidence levels such as 99%) allow for a wide range of average scores to be counted as "proficient."

To see what this dynamic looks like in practice, consider a hypothetical data display for subgroup scores with confidence intervals such as those shown in Figure 5.1 (taken from Cawthon, 2008). The average (mean) scores for each group of students (118, 29, 17) are displayed along with the 95% confidence interval for those scores (the range surrounding the scores). The width of the confidence interval in its simplest form depends on the size of each group and the percentage achieving proficiency. In this example, the first group (mean score of 118) actually has the fewest members, resulting in a wider confidence interval than in the other two groups. This group therefore has a greater range of scores that would meet the state criteria for statistically meeting AYP. Although rare, an example of the range falling at or below 0% proficient is possible when confidence intervals are used with small sample sizes (Cawthon, 2008).

There are strengths and drawbacks to the use of confidence intervals. Strengths include the ability to incorporate sample size into the AYP criteria

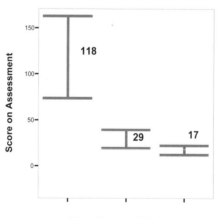

Figure 5.1. Confidence intervals reflecting scores for three groups of students. Adapted from "No Child Left Behind and Schools for the Deaf: Integration Into the Accountability Framework" by S. Cawthon, 2008, in R. C. Johnson and R. Mitchell (Eds.), *Testing Deaf Students in an Age of Accountability* (pp. 92–114), Washington, DC: Gallaudet University Press.

calculations, an important factor when considering the statistical properties of student proficiency measurement. A second strength is that benchmarks move from cutoff points to a target range of scores, which allows for greater flexibility in the accountability framework and enables schools or subgroups that are within statistically similar scores to receive a positive AYP designation. However, there are also some drawbacks to the use of confidence intervals, particularly when used in conjunction with very small group sizes. When the number of members in a group is very small, the confidence interval can span such a wide range that it renders the score and its interpretation meaningless.

Consider two examples from the state of Maryland, which uses confidence intervals and, because it has a small minimum group size of five students, sometimes applies confidence intervals to very small group sizes, which can create distortions. In the report card for the Frederick campus, the confidence interval for meeting AYP objectives in reading increases as the number of students per subgroup decreases. For the 2004 school year, Maryland had a target proficiency rate of 46.1% in reading. The overall Frederick school proficiency rate (n = 93 students) was 37% with a confidence interval of 21.9–47.3%. The school did not meet the target proficiency rate but did fall within the confidence interval, therefore meeting AYP requirements. This use reflects a reasonable use of confidence intervals that can be applied to large groups.

However, the subgroup analysis led to much wider confidence intervals. Two of the subgroups had fewer than 15 members, leading to very wide confidence intervals in AYP calculations. In one case, the percentage proficient for the group was 0%, but the confidence interval ranged from -11.7% to 80.9%. Although the group's proficiency rate fell within this range, it is difficult to say that they met the goal of 46.1% proficiency in reading for the year. This example is an extreme one, but it is given to illustrate an important point: when group sizes become so small that the confidence intervals spread across the entire range of possible outcomes, it is misleading to say that the subgroup has met AYP criteria. Improper use of the confidence interval can lead to an overestimation of student proficiency on state assessments. It is important, therefore, to consider group size, proficiency rates, and the use of confidence intervals when interpreting benchmark information on state report cards.

Recommendations for Action

There are a number of steps that can be taken to help improve the use of accountability frameworks for students who are deaf or hard of hearing. The recommendations in Chapter 4 focus on the kinds of measures used to evaluate student progress; these recommendations focus mainly on the reporting of that information. Specific recommendations for policy, research, and practice are described here.

The first policy recommendation echoes those made in the previous chapter: to aggregate the test scores of students who are deaf or hard of hearing, a low-incidence group, to the state level. Data reporting at the school level, except for the schools for the deaf, effectively buries information about the progress of students who are deaf or hard of hearing under the students with disabilities category. Within a state, scores for a school for the deaf with a report card do not represent the population of students who are deaf or hard of hearing within the state as a whole. As a result, too much attention paid may be paid to scores at the school for the deaf. Even if there are disputes about the content and format of assessment used in accountability reforms, having little to no information about how the group of students who are deaf or hard of hearing *as a whole* performs on state assessments is a detriment to all parties.

The second policy recommendation is for any future accountability reform to revise the set of consequences, or sanctions. The first recommended change is to have a set of "incentives" or "excellence recognition" categories for schools that make progress in meeting their educational goals. An approach that focuses only on the negative aspects of a school's performance creates an unhealthy relationship between teachers and administrative staff members, both at the school and the state levels. Schools are more than the results of a single test; current format penalizes an entire school if one group does not meet criteria in one subject in one grade. This form of evaluation is draconian, and demoralizing. The goal of "meeting AYP" as a school should be possible even if there is a relatively small number of subgroups that do not meet state goals. It may be best to remove the binary nature of the evaluation and go back to a relative ranking scale. For example, instead of "meet" versus "not meet," perhaps a percentage of goals met would provide a more accurate indication of school progress. Markers of excellence should also be based on other criteria in addition to the results of the statewide assessment. For example, the percentage of students who participate in service to the community may be a valuable way of tracking how the school helps to make connections between the student body and the surrounding community.

Third, the consequences themselves (i.e., school choice, supplemental services, changes to staff, and reconstitution of the school) are either arbitrary or based on ideas about "good" educational reform instead of on evidence that they result in meaningful improvement for students. The consequences should be constructive in nature, meant to strengthen the fabric of the school, instead of pull it apart. The consequences might therefore focus on action plans, parental input, and an authentic assessment of areas where teachers can better work with students who have traditionally been underserved in public education. There is research literature available from organizational psychology field and from the study of community change (Bracht et al., 1994; Speer & Hughey, 1995) that can form a stronger basis for decisions about consequences for schools. One potential policy change is to place the ownership of the criteria used to measure school success into the hands of the local leaders, teachers, parents, and students. Shifting the purpose of assessment results to a purpose that focuses on the utility of individual student data for instruction may also result in a change in chosen benchmarks and aggregated reports of student achievement. Drawing from the framework of IDEA, at least for students with disabilities, an approach to educational reform that is focused on progress goals for each student may be an appropriate place to start. In this way, the intent of the legislation and the actions behind it can be in alignment with the original intent of ESEA.

In a strong version of change, this proposed shift focuses less on meeting a uniform benchmark determined by the state and more on internal processes that respect the context of the individual school. This shift would give the power and ownership of the evaluation to the local level, creating an assessment system that informs the participants about their own progress in a way that builds capacity for change. Such an approach enables community members to identify and strive for excellence in a way that incorporates their own sense of identity and goals for the future. For example, administrators, teachers, parents, and students could work together to (a) identify goals;

(b) articulate steps on how to achieve those goals; and (c) mobilize resources to meet them, not only from the federal and state governments but also from the local community.

Options for mobilizing resources to meet goals have been constrained under NCLB. The NCLB approach to improvement, other than school closure, has been to provide funds for tutoring services and to allow some limited forms of school choice. The focus on instruction and on how to engage the community in school improvement has been more limited. In a holistic perspective, the view of resources available to help improve student performance goes beyond the teachers and the schools to include the families and communities where the students live. The current accountability system does not emphasize ways to build demonstrably needed capacities in local schools (Rebell & Wolff, 2008). Furthermore, local administration and teachers have had little to no input in the discussion about the kinds of resources that would help them raise student achievement. An incentive system that encourages collaboration with the community, within an accountability framework that has their input and buy-in, may result in school improvement plans that can integrate not only assessment results but also other community resources (a Deweyan "strong democratic" approach to NCLB proposed by Granger, 2008). Resultant efforts that reflect the needs of each school community may be more effective than a one-size-fits-all approach to school improvement.

This major undertaking is necessary because benchmark goals for standardized assessment test scores do not intrinsically motivate individuals to succeed. While it may encourage administrators and teachers to provide supplementary tutoring, use practice test items instead of implementing classroom activities, or even teach to the test, this process does not instill a love of learning or ownership over one's own success (Gratz, 2000; Herman & Golan, 1993; Hess & Brigham, 2000; Ketter & Pool, 2001). Changing the lens of assessment would increase intrinsic motivation to succeed and potentially reduce the many costs of implementing NCLB. The more important goal, however, would be to have school and district communities identify their own goals for success that reflect the identities and vision of the community's members. *Schools for the deaf are strong communities built around a common language and culture; incorporating their identity and collective efficacy would be an important step toward humanizing the NCLB assessment process and perhaps making the assessment process more meaningful, overall.* High standards would still be emphasized, but not in a one-size-fits-all formula that ignores the context of the individual student and school system and what we know about individual differences in how students who are deaf or hard of hearing learn (Hardman & Dawson, 2008).

In contrast to research recommendations in Chapter 4 that emphasize empirical measures of the effects of accommodations, this research recommendation follows a more qualitative approach. The following central questions are ones that I believe need to be more fully understood: What effects do accountability reforms have on communities that surround students who are deaf or hard of hearing? How do the cultural and linguistic backgrounds of students who are deaf or hard of hearing and the Deaf community interact with accountability reforms? Accountability reform is inherently an externally driven mechanism to enact change within the education system. Yet a child's world (indeed, the world for each of us) is broader than the classroom. What we do, say, think, and feel outside of school has a direct impact on how we experience education. Educational reforms that are applied to a culturally diverse and rich context, without understanding how those within that context interact with that policy, are likely to be ineffective at best and destructive at worst. We need to explore, from a culturally embedded perspective, how issues such as content standards, student assessment, and school report cards affect students who are deaf or hard of hearing. Do they inspire change in instructional strategies? Do they involve parents in partnership with teachers? Do they allow students to learn the language skills they need while they gain knowledge in core content areas? Answers to these questions are particularly important to know given the diversity of student, school, and community characteristics. Whereas a low-incidence population stands as a challenge to large-scale, quantitative studies, it is not a large obstacle to conducting quality interviews or observational research. Change for students who are deaf and hard of hearing, in and of itself, is not meaningful unless it is rooted in a deep understanding of (a) what is happening in the deaf education community with regard to accountability reform and (b) how to leverage the strengths of both to result in better outcomes for students who are deaf or hard of hearing.

Considering the practice domain, accountability reform is a policy that, as it stands, gives only cursory attention to instructional practice, which does not mean, however, that it does not have an impact on how teachers teach or what students who are deaf or hard of hearing learn. One of the challenges for students who are deaf or hard of hearing is that their progress, with the exception of some schools for the deaf, is rarely clearly apparent. Instead, data about their progress are combined with that of students with other disabilities, often a group with characteristics quite different from their own. The first practice recommendation is for teachers in regular education settings: resist the temptation to determine whether your students who are deaf or hard of hearing fall into the category of "bubble kid," and respond to the needs of each student. If the student is in a regular education classroom without additional support, it is likely that she is close to or at grade level in some of her subjects. However, to gain a sense of perspective on the student's achievement relative to other students who are deaf or hard of hearing, the teacher may find it helpful to have that student participate in the SAT-HI test or other agreed on assessment with deaf or hard of hearing norms. As a current example, the SAT-HI provides national norms for achievement for students with hearing loss. This information, along with district benchmarks, may give some helpful guidance in planning goals for the coming year. If possible, teachers should include multiple measures of student performance in an IEP or, if the student does not have one, in a portfolio of progress for the students' parents and future teachers.

The second recommendation is for parents who might be reviewing school report cards in choosing a school for their child who is deaf or hard of hearing. One of the claims of accountability reform is that it provides parents with needed information in choosing a school. Ideally, one could look at the report card, see whether the school has a track record of success in meeting school benchmarks, and then make an informed decision. Unfortunately, for students who are deaf or hard of hearing, meaningful information is not typically available in the standard report card format. Parents will need to do additional homework, much of it at the school itself, to be able to determine whether the school is prepared to teach their students who are deaf or hard of hearing. School and district administrators, or even local parent groups, could provide critical information about their previous successes in working with students who are deaf or hard of hearing. For example, graduation rates, postsecondary options, teachers with awards for excellence, and testimonials from students who are deaf or hard of hearing about their experiences would be very valuable information to new parents seeking information about the school. All educational settings would benefit from having this kind of "accountability" information ready for new parents. In the end, a proactive, informative approach might remove a small bit of the negativity placed on schools by NCLB.

Conclusion

The effectiveness of accountability as an educational reform will lie in the extent to which it improves student achievement. A fair and equitable accountability framework relies on a strong foundation of standards and assessment. Once established, accountability policies can then use this information to leverage external encouragement and/or pressure to change (and perhaps improve) student learning. This chapter focused on the schools as the target "unit of accountability." Out of the variety of educational structures that serve students who are deaf or hard of hearing, the schools for the deaf are the most visible participants in school-based accountability reforms.

As this discussion demonstrates, the reality of accountability truly reflects the old saying that "the devil is in the details." When accountability moves from the broad, theoretical constructs to how choices are made about evaluating schools, there are many factors at play. These factors affect schools for the deaf in very specific ways. Because students who are deaf or hard of hearing are a low-incidence population, it is only at these schools where we can see a local measure of how students fare on state assessments. These schools are also the only venues where students with hearing loss are fully reflected through a school's report card and AYP status. The details of accountability, however, including minimum group size and confidence intervals, make it much less likely that we will know a great deal about gains in student achievement, especially for this group, as a result of accountability reforms. The true impact at a local level of NCLB measures or similarly designed measures is far less transparent than the original large-scale approach would predict. Although the broad swaths of accountability reform have a large impact on administrators and teachers, the percentage of deaf and hard of hearing students for which schools, districts, and states are directly "held accountable" is quite small. Contextual factors such as the diversity of the school and how a state implements federal policy have a greater impact on whether a school or district faces consequences for student achievement than student performance on state assessments. It is possible that accountability reform can be changed so it includes incentives for all educational systems that serve students who are deaf or hard of hearing. In the meantime, the few schools for the deaf who do receive report cards and AYP grades will bear the brunt of accountability reform efforts.

6

Educational Professionals
and Accountability Reform

Chapter 6 turns to a different area of accountability reforms, those components that relate to educator skills and qualifications. Compared with curriculum standards and student assessment, measurement of teacher performance
is a relatively new aspect of accountability reform. Although teachers are intimately involved in, and ultimately responsible for, much of what happens
in the classroom, very few measures of teacher accountability are included in
most evaluations of school effectiveness (Moe, 2003). At the heart of teacher
accountability is the concept of teacher quality. *Teacher quality* can refer to
many things, ranging from an individual's credential status to the level of
student learning that results from classroom instruction. Teacher quality is a
highly politicized field, with long-standing disagreements about best practices
in teaching, teaching as a profession, teacher preparation programs, attributes
of an excellent teacher, and how to recruit and retain effective teachers in
hard-to-staff schools (e.g., Billingsley, 2004; Cochran-Smith, 2001; Darling-
Hammond & Sykes, 2003; Fulton, Yoon, & Lee, 2005; Ingersoll, 1998;
Temin, 2002; Zeichner, 1999). Educator-centered accountability reform is
thus done within the context of a highly contested arena.

Accountability and Teacher Quality Guidelines

NCLB introduced new criteria for states, districts, and schools with regard to teacher qualifications and certification, stirring a new round of debate on how to improve instruction by means of teacher preparation policies. The law used the term "Highly Qualified" to describe teachers who were allowed to teach in public schools. The purpose of the teacher quality aspect of accountability is to encourage schools and districts to hire and retain teachers who meet prescribed quality standards. Similar to the history behind curricular content area standards, teacher quality provisions draw on the standards-based reforms of the 1980s and 1990s. Under the current version of accountability reform, the definition of a "Highly Qualified" teacher focuses mainly on credentialing and certification:

- Teachers at all levels are to have a bachelor's degree.
- Teachers at all levels are to pass a state examination in their subject area (or areas).
- Teachers at all levels are to hold a license to teach in their state.
- Teachers at the middle/secondary level must demonstrate coursework or degree completion in the subject area that they teach.
- Teachers who have a temporary, provisional, or emergency certification are not considered "Highly Qualified."

These guidelines, with state certification being only one component of the requirements for a Highly Qualified teacher, are a step above the status quo where, at the time of passage, there were less rigorous requirements for subject area certification and a more liberal use of temporary certifications (Walsh, 2004). The focus of the NCLB guidelines was on teachers who teach in core academic areas: English, reading, math, science, foreign languages, social studies, and arts. Whereas teachers in the elementary grades are not evaluated on a single subject area, teachers in middle or high school must show competency in the specific courses that they teach. The emphasis on content area mastery is important because most teachers have a master's degree in education but do not have specialized content area expertise (Angrist & Guryan, 2004). Under this framework, an education degree without either supporting coursework or a degree in a subject area would not be sufficient for middle or high school teachers (Henig, 2006).

The teacher quality guidelines were to be phased in over the course of the first four years of the law. Very few states met the initial criteria, and some struggled to bring this aspect of NCLB accountability online (Education Commission of the States, 2004; Feller, 2006). In 2006–07, every teacher in a Title I school had to meet the minimum standards outlined above, though state plans have included provisions that add leniency in how they are met (Porter-Magee, 2004). For example, states were allowed to classify teachers as Highly Qualified if they were *enrolled* in an alternative certificate program, even if they had not completed it or passed a state test (Darling-Hammond & Sykes, 2003). Once again, state implementation of a federal accountability law has a significant impact on how it affects schools and districts.

NCLB purports that the law's Highly Qualified standards reflect attributes of teachers who will provide a quality education. At the heart of this kind of teacher quality reform is the assumption that stronger teacher certification standards will result in better teachers (Kleinhenz & Ingvarson, 2004). Just as standards-based reform focused on what the students should be learning, legislation concerning teacher quality focuses on the standards for teacher *preparation* (Dean, Lauer, & Urquhart, 2005). The assumed connection between Highly Qualified teacher standards and student achievement is shown in Figure 6.1.

This connection between Highly Qualified teacher preparation standards and student achievement is based on research that shows that teacher characteristics and teaching effectiveness have potentially significant impacts on student achievement (e.g., Darling-Hammond & Youngs, 2002; Odden, Borman, & Fermanich, 2004; Porter, 1989, 2002). This approach also assumes that the reason students struggle to reach high levels of student achievement is because of deficits in the teaching force (Greenwood & Maheady, 1997; Ingersoll, 2005). The approach is also more specific than approaches that

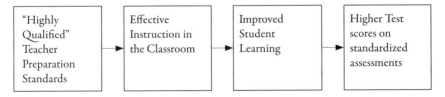

Figure 6.1. Assumed link between "Highly Qualified" teacher standards and student achievement.

have looked at teacher salaries or scores on certification exams as predictors of student achievement—research that has led to few consistent conclusions (Hanushek & Rivkin, 2004; Sable & Hill, 2006). The degree to which teachers are deemed responsible for student outcomes can focus efforts toward improving teacher effectiveness but can also lead to a blame game (Darling-Hammond, 2000; Greenwood, 1991; Porter-Magee, 2004; Soar, Medley, & Coker, 1983). One of the reasons that the NCLB guidelines are controversial is that they put a large focus on the ability of teachers to produce stronger student outcomes regardless of student background, student preparation, or other mitigating factors (Freedman, 2006; Hanushek, 2001a, 2001b; Walsh, 2004).

Recall that NCLB is a reauthorization of the ESEA, part of President Johnson's War on Poverty initiative. With this additional focus on teacher qualifications, NCLB attempts to address not only the financial inequities in education but also the "instructor gap" (Peske & Haycock, 2006). Students from low-income families, those in special education, or those who are English Language Learners continue to be more likely to have an underprepared or novice teacher than their peers (The Center for the Future of Teaching and Learning, 2006). In this articulation, *equity* is an important theme in the NCLB text on teacher quality:

> Equity Plans—States must have a plan in place to ensure that poor or minority children are not taught by inexperienced, unqualified, or out-of-field teachers at higher rates than are other children. [ESEA §1111(b)(8)(C)]

Issues of equity are often conceptualized as a problem of uneven distribution wherein experienced, certified teachers are found more in wealthy schools (Darling-Hammond & Sykes, 2003). This imbalance results in a disproportionate percentage of teachers without sufficient qualifications in schools that serve students from high-poverty neighborhoods (Peske & Haycock, 2006). Because there is not an organizational structure in place for allocating high-quality teachers to students who have the greatest need, the opposite placement occurs. Good teachers move to districts and schools with better support systems, salaries, and resources. As a result, according to Ladson-Billings in an American Educational Research Association presidential address, we have more than an achievement gap; we have an education debt to pay:

[I see] some metaphorical concurrences between our national fiscal situation and our education situation. I am arguing that our focus on the achievement gap is akin to the focus on the budget deficit, but what is actually happening to African-American, Latino, Asian-American immigrants and Native American students is really more like the national debt. We do not have an achievement gap. We have an education debt. (Ladson-Billings, 2006)

Can accountability reform use extrinsic measures to increase the proportion of prepared, highly skilled teachers in high-poverty schools? From an economic standpoint, products are priced according to the twin factors of supply and demand (Angrist & Guryan, 2004; Temin, 2002). Accountability reforms address supply and demand for teachers through external pressures exerted on school and district administrators. These reforms are designed to address supply through policies that define ways that teachers can be certified to teach. In tandem, accountability reforms are designed to affect demand by requiring all schools to be staffed with teachers who meet Highly Qualified standards.

There is emerging evidence that teachers do have an impact on how well students fare in accountability reform. High school seniors in California now face a high school exit exam to earn a high school diploma; students in schools with underprepared teachers were less likely to pass the state exit exam than those in schools with fully prepared teachers (The Center for the Future of Teaching and Learning, 2006). In further support of this approach, there is some research evidence that teachers who come from university teacher education programs and are fully licensed by the state are more successful with students than teachers who go through other types of preparation programs (Darling-Hammond & Cobb, 1996). Although effective teaching is a complex combination of teacher characteristics and background (Cochran-Smith & Lytle, 1990; Corcoran, Evans, & Schwab, 2004), NCLB policymakers have taken the emphasis on *subject matter teacher preparation* to heart with the Highly Qualified teacher standards (Kupermintz, 2002).

The above assumptions about teacher quality and its impact on student achievement can be applied directly to students who are deaf or hard of hearing (see Figure 6.2). This application draws, in part, from the literature on competencies of educators of students who are deaf or hard of hearing (discussed later in this chapter). Two things are notable about this adapted list: (a) teacher preparation standards and areas of effective classroom instruction

Higher Teacher Preparation Standards *that cover communication, primary and/or secondary grade level subject matter knowledge, history and Deaf culture, working with diverse student population, and technology.*	Effective Instruction in the Classroom *that facilitates language and literacy development, self-advocacy, social and emotional development, whether in specialized programs or inclusive settings.*	Improved Student Learning in *both literacy and core content areas, improved preparation for higher education.*	Higher Test scores on standardized assessments, *higher high school graduation rates, and career outcomes.*

Figure 6.2. Assumed link between teacher quality standards and student achievement for students who are deaf or hard of hearing.

is described with a great deal of specificity; content knowledge about teaching students who are deaf or hard of hearing is needed in addition to pedagogical skills in academic content areas (Easterbrooks, 1991) and (b) the outcomes are expanded to address issues of concern in the Deaf community, specifically the transition between high school and postsecondary opportunities. As some states implement reforms where all students are required to pass state exit exams to receive a high school diploma, scores on standardized tests have implications not only for school accountability but also for student employability.

The pathway in Figure 6.2 assumes that the reason why some students who are deaf or hard of hearing have struggled academically is due, *at least in part*, to the inadequacy of instruction and the learning environment (Porter-Magee, 2004). This assumption represents a "teacher-deficit" explanation for low levels of student achievement (Ingersoll, 2005). The idea is that teacher preparation programs have not, to date, provided instructors with the tools needed to establish communication pathways that facilitate grade-level knowledge and skills (Johnson, 2003b; Levine, 2006; Walsh, 2004; for a discussion of research activity by faculty in deaf education programs, see Schirmer, 2008). The focus on teacher preparation standards and on professional development programs is in response to the teacher-deficit assumption.

The following section of this chapter looks more closely at the teacher preparation programs that train professionals who serve students who are deaf or hard of hearing.

Highly Qualified Teachers in Special Education

Many students who are deaf or hard of hearing learn in classrooms taught by teachers trained to educate students with disabilities. Teachers may have certification either as teachers of the deaf or as special education teachers who work with students from a range of backgrounds. Regulations for teacher preparation come from similar sources as other areas of accountability reform. Both NCLB and the reauthorized Individuals With Disabilities Education Improvement Act of 2004 emphasize standards for both teacher qualifications and student performance. Although special education and regular education traditionally followed separate paths, changes in the last few decades have brought the two practices increasingly more in parallel with each other (Blanton et al., 2003; Council for Exceptional Children, 2001; Schrag, 2003). Accountability components have become explicitly integrated into the framework for providing specialized services for students with disabilities. The language of accountability is now articulated as part of IDEA, increasing the likelihood that these policy changes will last even if they fade in reauthorizations of NCLB. Teacher preparation standards form the basis of what knowledge and skills teachers bring into the classroom. What do the criteria of a Highly Qualified teacher mean for special education? What do they mean for those who teach students who are deaf or hard of hearing? More importantly, do these guidelines serve to reduce the instructor gap that contributes to low levels of academic achievement for students who are deaf or hard of hearing?

Under NCLB, teachers in special education are largely held to the same teacher quality standards as teachers in regular education, with additional requirements for certification in teaching students with disabilities. For the purpose of teacher accountability, teachers of the deaf are treated in the same way as special education teachers. For example, if the teacher provides instruction in a core academic area, he or she must meet the Highly Qualified standards for that subject area in addition to required certification in special education. For elementary level teachers, required certification includes passing a state exam in relevant subject areas. For middle and high school teachers, requirements include demonstrating coursework or degree completion in the core academic area taught. For example, a high school teacher who teaches physics and biology would need to have separate certification for each subject area. For those teachers who teach multiple subjects, states are working on a single process to gain approval in all areas in a streamlined process.

There are some significant implications for special educators who do not have subject-area certification. If teachers do not meet the core academic subject requirement, they must coteach with another teacher who does meet these guidelines (Education Commission of the States, 2004). Figure 6.3 is a helpful flowchart of the various roles of special educators and their requirements under NCLB (Council for Exceptional Children, 2005). Teachers in rural schools (defined in Title 6 of NCLB) had an extension until the end of the 2007–08 academic year to meet these requirements for core academic areas (Council for Exceptional Children, 2005).

The flowchart begins with four IDEA-related roles that are not covered by accountability, basically, serving students who are either in early childhood development programs or outside of core academic areas. If the educational professional is not exclusively serving students in one of these two ways, then he or she is exempt from accountability standards. Essentially, if the teacher is working with (a) students in a core content area and (b) students who will later participate in state standardized assessments, then the teacher is subject to Highly Qualified standards. Although this chart may make it appear that there are many exemptions to the Highly Qualified rules, the majority of teachers will fall into the lower right hand side of the flowchart that states certification requirements to meet accountability guidelines.

The purpose of a special educator is to ensure that the learning context is accessible for students with disabilities and that the IEP requirements are implemented as planned. This role is essential because it is part of how schools can provide free and appropriate public education for students with disabilities under IDEA. For example, students with disabilities often need additional practice on a skill beyond what is routinely provided in the general curriculum. A special educator can facilitate learning by helping a student prepare in advance of instruction or by reinforcing instruction already provided in the regular education classroom.

With the emphasis on inclusive classroom instruction, special educators frequently work in collaboration with regular education teachers (Kassini,

IDEA & NCLB Special Education "Highly Qualified" Requirements

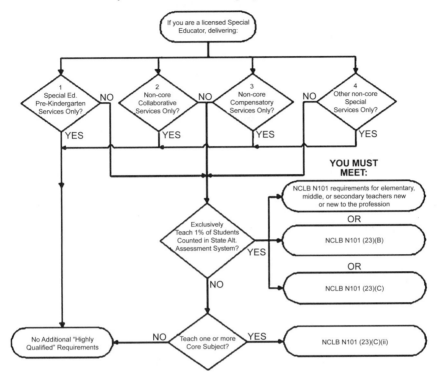

Figure 6.3. Flowchart showing IDEA and NCLB resources for "Highly Qualified" requirements for special educators. From *Resources on "Highly Qualified" Requirements for Special Educators*, by Council for Exceptional Children, 2005, p. 6. Copyright 2005 by Council for Exceptional Children.

2008; Lee-Tarver, 2006; Scruggs & Mastropieri, 1996). When two or more teachers are responsible for planning, instructing, and evaluating content knowledge, there may be some confusion as to who needs to meet what requirements under NCLB. The distinction will be between teachers who take on a *primary* role in providing core subject instruction and those teachers who provide *consultative* services. Consultative services are defined in the following way:

> A special education teacher who provides only consultative services to a highly qualified teacher . . . should be considered a highly qualified special education teacher if such teacher meets the requirements of Section 602(10)(A). Such consultative services do not include instruction in core academic subjects but

may include adjustments to the learning environment, modifications of instructional methods, adaptation of curricula, the use of positive behavioral supports and interventions, or the design, use or implementation of appropriate accommodations to meet the needs of individual children. (H. Report 779, 108th Cong., 2nd Session 171, IDEIA, 2004)

One potential unintended consequence of teacher quality measures is a shift in the role of special educators, including teachers of the deaf, from one of collaboration to consultation. For students in the middle and high school grades, special educators without requisite subject area certification will not be allowed to take on primary instruction for students in those core academic areas, which will necessarily shift the emphasis of primary instruction into the regular education classroom. Although special educators without subject area certification may have previously provided academic instruction in a pull-out setting, accountability reform measures now eliminate this option. The push toward instruction by a person with core content area certification may especially change the role of special educators in secondary settings. Instead of a coteaching arrangement, special educators may be asked to play a consultative role in how core academic area content is taught to students with disabilities. The focus may shift even more toward reinforcement of taught material and generalization of newly acquired skills and away from direct content area instruction. The special educator would likely be responsible for implementation of IEP strategies and the method of instruction rather than the content of instruction (Council for Exceptional Children, 2005; Schrag, 2003).

New accountability reform measures are being implemented just as the country is facing a shortage of public school teachers, especially those in special education. The availability of certified instructors has a direct effect on a school or district's ability to hire and retain teachers who meet quality standards (Billingsley, 2004; Ingersoll, 2001). Teacher shortages are far more acute in the fields of special education, English as a Second Language, or bilingual education than they are for regular education (American Association for Employment in Education, 2003; Darling-Hammond & Sykes, 2003; Mc-Cleskey, Tyler, & Flippin, 2004; Ralabate, 2006). Potentially, increasing numbers of graduates who have taken alternate routes to certification might bring in more teachers, but these numbers remain small in relation to the staffing needs across the country (Feistritzer, 2005a, 2005b; Honawar, 2006; Muller,

2005a; North Central Regional Educational Laboratory, 2002; Rosenberg & Sindelar, 2005). Reports from the field indicate that school and district administrators do not have strong pools of applicants to choose from when hiring new special educators (Toplikar, 2006). This shortage is particularly acute when looking at culturally and linguistically diverse teachers in special education (Miller, Strosnider, & Dooley, 2002; Webb-Johnson, Artiles, Trent, Jackson, & Velox, 1998).

Related to recruitment, one of the greatest challenges facing special education is keeping the teachers who are already in the field (Boe, Bobbitt, & Cook, 1997). The turnover rate for special educators is higher than in other fields (Ingersoll, 2001). A school with a high turnover rate can find it challenging to maintain the free and appropriate public education guidelines of IDEA (Brownell, Sindelar, Bishop, Langley, & Seo, 2002). The problem is especially acute for novice teachers; special education teachers are most likely to leave within the first five years of teaching. Furthermore, teachers without full certification are twice as likely to leave the classroom as those with certification (Boe, Barkanic, & Leow, 1999). These factors, taken together, suggest that teachers who are underprepared or who have less experience are more likely to leave the profession than those who are more experienced and are fully accredited. Accountability reforms that focus on teacher preparation may therefore be an effective way to increase the supply of teachers working in special education, but they do less to address the turnover rate once teachers enter the profession (Fulton et al., 2005; Rosenberg & Sindelar, 2005; Schrag, 2003; Steffan, 2004).

Teachers of Students Who Are Deaf or Hard of Hearing

Issues of supply and demand also apply to teachers of students who are deaf or hard of hearing. As with special education as a whole, there is a significant, and growing, lack of teachers prepared to work with deaf and hard of hearing students (Johnson, 2003b; LaSasso & Wilson, 2000; Muller, 2005b). Although the number of deaf or hard of hearing students who receive services has increased by roughly 20% in the 1990s, the number of teachers who are prepared to teach them has remained the same (Johnson, 2003b). University teacher preparation programs in deaf education are also threatened to close due to low enrollment (Moores, 2004). From a cultural competency stand-point, there are very few teachers who are Deaf themselves or who reflect the growing diversity of students who are deaf or hard of hearing (Andrews & Jordan, 1993; Martin & Lytle, 2000; Ramsey, 1997). There are many challenges that face teacher preparation and retention effort in deaf education, including (a) gaps in our knowledge about the qualifications of teachers who work with students who are deaf or hard of hearing, (b) the retention rate of these teachers, (c) their effectiveness, and (d) questions about how to recruit new teachers who are prepared to teach students from a diverse background (Johnson, 2003a). The controversial issues in regular education with respect to teacher quality are thus even more heightened when applied to educating students who are deaf or hard of hearing (Steffan, 2004).

There is little information on how many teachers of the deaf meet the Highly Qualified teacher certification standards. It is possible, drawing from anecdotal evidence, that the rate of teachers who do not meet guidelines may be higher than the rest of special education due to the relatively few teacher preparation programs available to prospective teachers (Johnson, 2003b). Only a handful of schools for the deaf use the AYP report card as a mechanism for informing the public about teacher qualifications (Cawthon, 2007); more may begin doing so as the requirements for 100% Highly Qualified teachers comes to pass. For the school report cards available from the 2004–05 school year (Cawthon, 2008), only three schools report information about teacher background. Alaska and Louisiana report "percentage of classes taught by highly qualified teachers" (0% and 47%, respectively). The Governor Baxter School for the Deaf in Maine reported educational attainment of staff members. Within the school, 68% of the instructional staff members held a master's degree compared with the state average of 36%. For instructional support staff members, the figures were higher: 100% of instructional support staff members at the school had a master's degree compared with 82% of similar professionals at the state level. Although this information is not put into the context of teacher quality standards of NCLB, it does provide some perspective on the level of training of the schools' staff members.

The implications of teacher quality measures are partially tied to educational setting and the varying roles of educators who serve students who are deaf or hard of hearing (Bodner-Johnson & Martin, 1999; Kassini, 2008). As discussed in Chapter 1, students who are deaf or hard of hearing are diverse, and so are the settings where they learn. In schools for the deaf or in programs where students receive primary academic instruction in separate settings, teachers of the deaf play a significant role. In contrast, students in mainstream settings may receive only supplemental services from itinerant teachers of the deaf, being provided the bulk of content area instruction by general education teachers (Kluwin, Morris, & Clifford, 2004; Muller, 2005a). In this mainstream scenario, a teacher of the deaf will have intermittent contact with the students who are deaf or hard of hearing and their teachers to provide support services (Foster & Cue, 2009). The services of itinerant teachers are essential to providing a free and appropriate public education because regular education teachers are largely untrained in working with students with disabilities (Gaetano, 2006). Mainstream settings may also have special education teachers serving students with a range of disabilities, including students who are deaf or hard of hearing.

The collaborative nature of services for students who are deaf or hard of hearing is perhaps nowhere more formalized than in the creation and implementation of the IEP. The strength of a student's program will be, in part, due to the strength of the IEP team members. Yet there is concern about the preparation that educational professionals have to serve both the academic and language/communication needs of students who are deaf or hard of hearing (Dolman, 2008). There are legal ramifications for the quality of an IEP because the IEP is a central component of how a student's rights and opportunities as guaranteed through IDEA are formulated, documented, and evaluated. The IEP is also a critical tool in how free and appropriate public education is actualized in a manner that is tailored to the student's specific strengths and areas of need. As discussed in Chapter 4, the reauthorization of IDEA in 2004 requires that a child's IEP must include measurable benchmarks of academic progress and documentation on what instructional and assessment accommodations the student may need to meet those goals. The content of the IEP plan is developed collaboratively between the student, parents, teachers, and relevant professionals such as a speech/language therapist, interpreter, school psychologist, etc. A quality IEP process thus includes regular participation by professionals other than the main classroom teachers.

While the main part of the debate about NCLB teacher quality focuses on classroom teachers, there are also guidelines that affect paraeducators who might work with students who are deaf or hard of hearing. Paraeducators are the teacher aides and instructional assistants who assist with classroom instruction, most specifically in special education. Before the 1997 revision of IDEA, paraeducators did not receive systematic training or certification. Under NCLB, paraeducators had to meet the following standards:

- Completed 2 years of coursework beyond high school (48–60 hours)
- Have an associate's degree OR
- Demonstrated knowledge and skill on a state or local assessment

For many paraeducators in the field, these new guidelines will require additional coursework (Wall, Davis, Crowley, & White, 2005). For years, paraeducators have taken on greater instructional and classroom management responsibilities, increasing their need for teacher training and support. Formal programs such as ParaMet, help paraeducators gain the coursework and training they need to be NCLB compliant and to strengthen them as resources for special education students (Wall et al., 2005). The ParaMet program bases its curriculum on the Council for Exceptional Children's list of competencies for paraeducators (Council for Exceptional Children, 2005b). These standards range from knowing about the philosophy of special education to understanding instructional strategies, basic data collection techniques, and how to collaborate with other members of the IEP team (including parents).

Although outside the specific guidelines of NCLB, other educational professionals play a critical role in creating access for students who are deaf or hard of hearing. For students who use American Sign Language or other signed language, educational interpreters are one way that mainstreamed settings seek to create a free and appropriate public education that is consistent with the goals of IDEA. When provided under IDEA guidelines, an interpreter helps the school and the IEP to do the following:

> *(iv) Consider the communication needs of the child, and in the case of the child who is deaf or hard of hearing, consider the language and communication needs, opportunities for direct communication with peers and professionals in the child's language and communication mode, academic level, and full range of needs including opportunities for direct instruction in the child's language and communication mode, and (v) Consider whether the child requires assistive communication devices and services.* [IDEA Sec. 1414 (d) (3) (B)]

Educational interpreters have an extremely challenging task. Depending on the primary language of the child, an educational interpreter may translate teacher (and peer) English into American Sign Language, Signed Exact English, or other signed system. When interpreting during class time, educational interpreters must translate what the teacher says while at the same time ensuring that the student is paying attention. Monitoring student engagement is important in their role in providing access for the deaf student. If the student's proficiency in signed language is low or if she has not been trained in how to use an interpreter, then the student will not have access to classroom instruction (Stinson & Antia, 1999). The interpreter can provide a great deal of information to the IEP team about student attention and comprehension of interpreted material.

Interpreter quality is truly essential to the success of students who are deaf in mainstreamed settings. Without accurate and comprehensive interpretation of teacher instructions, students do not have an opportunity to learn material that is later assessed on state tests. Furthermore, the interpreter often acts as a mediator between the hearing-centered school setting and the Deaf world of the student (Shaw & Roberson, 2009), though, at times, she plays that role with limited Deaf cultural knowledge (McDermid, 2009). The role of educational interpreters has increased as students have moved into the mainstreamed settings and away from schools where the instructors are fluent in sign language. There are a few objective measures of interpreter proficiency, including certifications from the National Association of the Deaf, the Registry of Interpreters for the Deaf, and the Educational Interpreter Performance Assessment (EIPA) (Schick & Williams, 2001). Individuals who take the EIPA test are evaluated on a Likert scale of 0 to 5 on which 0 = no skills demonstrated and 5 = advanced native-like skills. These scores translate into a system of skill levels that range from Beginner to Advanced. A score of 3.5 or above is the minimum qualification for an interpreter to work within the school system.[1] The EIPA is currently used as part of the certification process in 21 states throughout the country. Yet few states have legislation regulating the standards for a quality interpreter (e.g., Sections 3051.16 and 3065 of

---

1. See the Classroom Interpreting Web site http://www.classroominterpreting.org, particularly, the page for the Educational Interpreter Performance Test, frequently asked questions about the rating system and certification.

Title 5 of the California Code of Regulations, amended July 2008; Registry of Interpreters for the Deaf, 2009). When discussing the preparedness of educational interpreters, information about certification or EIPA scores may come into play.

Recommendations for Action

Policy, research, and practice recommendations for action in teacher (or educator) quality are more intertwined than recommendations in the previous chapters. Accountability reform's emphasis on defining teacher quality through standards for teacher preparation is one approach to improving instruction and, by extension, student achievement. Yet the broad strokes of accountability reform may not be sufficiently flexible to improve student outcomes for those with unique educational needs. Students who are deaf or hard of hearing are served by educators in a variety of capacities, some with overlapping roles. In other words, separating educational professionals into those who provide "core content area" instruction and "consultative" instruction may not be appropriate for teachers with specialized training for educating these students (Pagliaro, 1998). Rather than set a goal to make all teachers meet the same standards, *it may be more appropriate to set a goal to have everyone be highly qualified in their specific roles and competencies in instruction for students who are deaf or hard of hearing.*

The next recommendation is for education administrators at the district and state level. This chapter discussed the need for equity plans for students who have been previously underserved in the public education community. I think it is necessary for schools to have an equity plan not only for students from ethnically and racially diverse backgrounds but also for students with disabilities. Teacher shortages are a significant issue in deaf education and threaten the ability of schools to provide a free and appropriate public education, which is required under IDEA. A simple extension of the ESEA language provides adequate motivation for such a goal:

> Equity Plans—States must have a plan in place to ensure that *students who are deaf or hard of hearing* are not taught by inexperienced, unqualified, or out-of-field teachers at higher rates than are other children. [ESEA §1111(b)(8)(C)] (emphasis added)

For such a plan to work, it is necessary to monitor who teaches students who are deaf or hard of hearing and then determine whether they are experienced, qualified, and have sufficient background to work with students who are deaf or hard of hearing. This approach brings the recommendation for a more comprehensive measure of teacher quality full circle: once a measure is in place for teacher quality, then equity for students who are deaf or hard of hearing in terms of their access to quality teachers becomes the foremost goal.

The first recommendation stems directly from how NCLB defines "Highly Qualified" in teacher accountability reforms. Although the credentialing process is certainly a part of building a strong teacher workforce, it is my recommendation that accountability efforts measure teacher quality in a more comprehensive manner than is currently in the definition of "Highly Qualified." In a sense, this recommendation echoes many recommendations in the assessment field suggesting that inferences about student achievement should not be made based on a single test score but, rather, on several contributing pieces of information. This line of thinking raises not only a question of what makes good measurement but also a question of what characteristics teachers of the deaf should have as they begin their careers. Teacher certification is, perhaps, only a starting point when thinking about what effective teaching looks like. For students who are deaf or hard of hearing, effective classroom instruction may go beyond a teacher's subject area credential and rest on proficiencies that are unique to serving this population (Foster & Cue, 2009). One task for the field is to draw on knowledge about successful education for students who are deaf or hard of hearing and to bring these specific criteria into the policy arena.

Preparation for educators of deaf or hard of hearing students has traditionally come from programs specifically designed to train teachers of the deaf. Yet the discussion here illustrates how very difficult it will be for such programs to remain focused on one group of educators among the broader set of professionals who serve this student population. It will continue to be challenging to attract new educators into the field with the shrinking number of programs that can offer the credentials that comply with accountability guidelines for teacher quality. I expect that there will be transition to a more broadly based training approach in terms of the type of credentials provided, with programs still maintaining the essential specialization skills needed to effectively serve students who are deaf or hard of hearing (e.g., the master's degree program described in Simms & Thumann, 2007). It will also be important for deaf education programs to connect with training programs for regular education teachers or special education teachers who will have students who are deaf or hard of hearing in their classrooms. The lack of expertise in these settings, and the increased number of students who begin schooling in mainstreamed classrooms, indicate a significant need for targeted resources and training.

Traditional training programs are housed within colleges and universities that provide degrees for full-time students who enter their programs soon after high school. There are some significant retraining needs for individuals such as paraeducators who may not have had this postsecondary experience. For example, Wall et al. (2005) recommend that schools and districts work with institutions of higher education to facilitate the kind of training that best supports the adult learner who has not had previous college course experience. Suggested actions include open enrollment policies for currently employed paraeducators; authentic learning experiences that are linked to their professional duties; and academic, writing, and study skill support to increase the likelihood that participants can complete their course requirements. Programs that prepare teachers of the deaf might consider creating outreach programs for paraeducators so they can gain the targeted skills needed to effectively serve students who are deaf or hard of hearing.

As noted several times in this chapter, one of the challenges in knowing the level of teacher quality of those who serve students who are deaf or hard of hearing lies in understanding what services they provide to students. Under an educational accountability reform framework, key questions remain: Who is providing core content area instruction? Do they meet Highly Qualified requirements (however they are defined)? This issue becomes especially critical for secondary teachers who work with students who are deaf or hard of hearing. Because most states certify teachers of students who are deaf or hard of hearing to teach at all grade levels, this group of teachers may have more challenges meeting the NCLB guidelines for core content area mastery than teachers from regular education preparation programs (Luckner, 1991, 1992). Teachers of the deaf who do not have a content area certification will no longer be allowed to teach a subject area such as math, reading, or science. Although teachers who held their positions before NCLB were allowed more flexibility in meeting Highly Qualified standards, teachers hired since that time (2002) were to follow the criteria outlined in the law. This directive is true for teachers who work in all educational settings and serve students with a wide range of characteristics and needs. Teachers in mainstreamed settings are less likely affected because there is typically a collaborative relationship between teachers with different backgrounds. Teachers at schools for the deaf, however, take primary responsibility for content area instruction. Teachers at schools for the deaf are thus more likely to need additional certification to meet Highly Qualified guidelines. These accountability reforms therefore target teacher preparation programs as much as they do individual teachers and schools.

Access assistants, specifically educational interpreters, have largely been left out of large-scale accountability reforms. There have, over the past several decades, been multiple calls for improvement in the quality of educational interpreting for students in mainstreamed settings (Jarvis, 2002; McCartney, 1994; Powers, 2001; Simms & Thumann, 2007). How to improve quality of educational interpreting is a pressing concern if students are to have equal access to the content of instruction. Accountability reforms, through their emphasis on academic proficiency, may therefore push the envelope on quality interpreting and, by implication, access to content area standards. So while the credentialing and quality of educational interpreters may not be articulated in NCLB, the fact that states and districts now report academic performance of students with disabilities may play a role in raising expectations for the quality of interpreting to which students have access.

Another practice recommendation is to continue to strengthen and expand teacher induction programs for teachers once they have reached the field—not only for teachers with a credential to work with students who are deaf or hard of hearing but also for special educators and regular education teachers. Induction can take the form of teacher mentorship, expanded professional development programs, and networking between new professionals. The low incidence of students who are deaf or hard of hearing makes creation of a sustainable program quite challenging. However, sustainability is truly critical to (a) using resources wisely, (b) disseminating new information about best practices, and (c) creating a critical mass of teachers who can be a resource to new professionals (many thanks to B. Schirmer for her thoughts on this issue). Although the focus of previous programs has been on connecting individuals and providing information, sustainability is a needed component in how induction programs are conceptualized and implemented (South East

Regional Resource Center, 2004). What infrastructure components are necessary to create a sustainable teacher induction program for students who are deaf or hard of hearing, particularly those in regular education settings? Although program administrators can likely draw on previous efforts, successful sustainability models may require the inclusion of experts from business or nonprofit administration during the planning process.

Conclusion

The purpose of this chapter was to discuss aspects of accountability reform that attempt to strengthen educational outcomes by focusing on certification processes for educational professionals. Students who are deaf or hard of hearing are served by a wide range of educational professionals, each with important and complementary roles. It is debatable the extent to which broad teacher quality criteria, designed from the perspective of accountability at the school, district, and state levels, can meet the needs of individual students with needs that are met by multiple parties. NCLB and IDEA have evolved to be closely aligned in the areas of measures of content area achievement and goals for student proficiency. The IEP, a cornerstone for how students who are deaf or hard of hearing receive services, is a critical tool in integrating the goals of the two reform efforts. In contrast, NCLB and IDEA are not designed to adequately address the different priorities of teacher preparation programs. More specifically, programs to prepare educators to work with students who are deaf or hard of hearing have often had a set of methods different from those who prepare regular education teachers. The ultimate goal of success for students is the same, but at times, the routes to that goal include different methods, advocacy needs, communication strategies, and balance of classroom activities. Who provides content area instruction in accountability reform is the defining feature of teacher quality measures in accountability reform. A challenge for the deaf education field is therefore how to *integrate* priorities for deaf and hard of students into this framework.

7

Accountability to Parents

Accountability reform for education is, in a general sense, undertaken on behalf of the taxpaying public. Elementary and secondary education is funded largely through public revenue, and as stakeholders, taxpayers are interested in the efficacy of public education. Some education reforms refine this concept of accountability to the public even more specifically: accountability to parents. Thus far in this book, the discussion of accountability has been in terms of what is measured (student proficiency on content area standards) and who is evaluated (students, teachers, and schools). This chapter views accountability from the other end of the transaction. What options do parents have in response to the results obtained in accountability reforms? To be accountable *to* someone or something implies that there is a responsibility not only to measure success but also to ultimately succeed. If the school system is not successful in its goals to educate students, then accountability reform gives parents a course of action to follow.

Chapter 7 considers how accountability reform provides parents with leverage for implementing change in the services their children receive. School choice is the primary option for parents under current accountability reform. The chapter begins with a discussion of the role of school choice in the United States and its role in U.S. accountability reforms. School choice is not a new policy, but its inclusion in NCLB means that it is now integrated into the larger school accountability framework. School choice, however, has only a tangential fit with the overall goals of ESEA, in general, and IDEA, in particular. In this context, what does school choice offer for parents of students who are deaf or hard of hearing?

School Choice Policies

School choice has had a long and controversial history in the United States (Colvin, 2004; National Education Association, 2006). Traditional school enrollment policies limit attendance to schools within a geographical boundary, usually based on where families live. School choice refers to policies that allow parents flexibility in where their children go to school. Depending on the specifications of the choice policy, parents may have the option to send their children to another public school within the district (interdistrict transfer) or to a private school within district boundaries (Tice, Chapman, Princiotta, & Bielick, 2006). The essential principle behind school choice is that students will have better educational opportunities if their parents have more options as to where their children attend school. This principle is similar to a free-market economy, where consumers select options that best fit their needs. If a product is of low quality, consumers will stop selecting that option. Applied to education, schools that do not facilitate academic success for their students will see parents choosing to enroll their children elsewhere.

The discussions around school choice bring many critical issues to the forefront of what will lead to academic success for students. Cities with comprehensive school choice programs, also known as voucher programs, have been started in a handful of locations, including Wisconsin (Milwaukee), Ohio (Cleveland), Vermont, Maine, and Washington, DC (federally funded by the DC School Choice Incentive Act of 2003). These voucher programs are designed to provide additional educational opportunities for low-income students. In the voucher programs, parents are given a "credit" for the cost of educating their child in the local school. The parent can then take that money and use it to pay for private school tuition, an expense often out of reach for low-income families. Advocates see school choice as a way for disadvantaged children to have access to the benefits of private education. Critics of school choice or voucher programs say that moving children out of public schools undermines the educational efforts in local communities and that it seeks to benefit private schools more than students themselves. Amid the controversy, additional cities that have initiated voucher programs have been sued by opposition groups and are awaiting decisions within their respective state courts (Alliance for School Choice, 2007).

School choice plays a supporting role in the current accountability legislation. Although a full version of school choice (i.e., one with vouchers for private schools) was part of an early conceptualization of NCLB, the final NCLB legislation offers school choice in a more limited context (Hess & Finn, 2004; Hochschild, 2003). Choice under NCLB does not include vouchers to private schools, but offers parents of Title I students options *within* their public school districts. (Vouchers for private school education may be reintroduced in a reauthorization of the law.) Depending on the current state and local policies, school choice under the auspice of accountability may bring small or large changes in what decisions parents can make about where their children enroll in school. In states and districts with school choice programs already in place or with high student mobility, the accountability-based options may bring only small changes to options for parents (Howell, 2004). However, in states and districts without school choice programs, the NCLB choice presents parents with options when their local school fails to meet annual benchmarks for student achievement (the path to school choice is outlined in Chapter 3).

In addition to measures of student academic achievement, schools are also held accountable for the level of violence on their campuses. The school safety provision has not received much attention but is a relatively new component of accountability reform. Through the Unsafe School Choice Option, NCLB includes additional provisions for school choice for students who attend schools with a constant threat of violence.[§] One important aspect of the way federal reforms are implemented at a local level is the flexibility states have to create their own definitions of "persistently dangerous." There has been a noticeable jump in the number of states that have made progress in developing clear definitions of what constitutes an unsafe school (Education

---

§ In addition to transfer options for students who attend a persistently dangerous school, school safety policies also allow victims of a criminal offense on school property to transfer to another school within the district (even if the school does not have a "persistently dangerous" rating), policies that therefore apply only to individual students and not to all students within a school. A victim of a violent crime can transfer to a safe school within 10 days of the incident (20 U.S.C. §7912).

Commission of the States, 2004). In 2003, only seven states were on track in developing these definitions. By 2004, all but one state could document progress in this area. Consistent definitions for school safety are the first step in ensuring school choice options for students who are subject to recurrent violence in their schools.

What does it take for a school to earn a rating as an unsafe school? A school that is "persistently dangerous" is defined in many different ways from state to state, but usually includes some of the following elements: incidents where police officers are called to the campus, assaults on faculty or students, use of a weapon, robbery, rape, murder, and kidnapping. A persistently dangerous school is one that falls into a defined state policy such as this one for North Carolina:

> A "persistently dangerous school" is a public school in which the conditions during the past two school years continually exposed its students to injury from violent criminal offenses and it is an elementary, middle or secondary public school in which a total of five or more violent criminal offenses were committed per 1000 students (0.5 or more per 100 students) in two consecutive school years. (North Carolina State Board of Education, n.d.)

Schools therefore earn this rating only if the offenses are frequent and sustained over at least a 2- and sometimes a 3-year time frame. Under this definition, bullying or violence off of school property (e.g., on the bus) are not considered in a school's safety rating (King, 2007). For those states that use a measure involving "percentage of offenses per student," the thresholds for percentage rates range from 1.5% (as above in North Carolina) to 6% (National Center on Education Statistics, 2006). Some states solicit input from parents and students as to their perspective on the safety of the school. In Florida, for example, a school can earn a designation of persistently dangerous if more than half of the survey respondents rate the school as being unsafe. In this way, Florida asks parents directly about their perception of the safety of their child's school.

There are some real consequences for schools that receive a violent school rating. As with labels of "needs improvement" or "failing school," receiving a label of "persistently dangerous" can be quite damaging for morale. Schools are also, in a sense, responsible for monitoring the safety on their own campuses. For example, parents must rely on individual school principals to follow state definitions for violent acts and to report accurate data so states can make needed designations in the interest of child safety (King, 2007). Districts are also responsible for notifying parents of their eligibility to transfer to a safe school and to implement transfers within 30 days (20 U.S.C. §7912). Both of these actions require trust on the part of parents and due diligence by administrators. Unfortunately, the school safety definitions and policies have not resulted in an increase in the number of schools that have received an unsafe rating since the start of NCLB. It is inconceivable that no concerns about school safety remain; this element of accountability reform has led to little improvement in school safety. A more deliberate effort to implement school safety measures will be needed to create the traction necessary for this component of NCLB to provide real options for students and parents in unsafe learning environments.

Our ability to evaluate the effectiveness of school choice as an overall reform strategy is limited because there are only a few publicly funded school choice and voucher programs with enough data to analyze their impact on student outcomes (Wright, Wright, & Heath, 2003). Few of the assumptions behind school choice have been tested in controlled, empirical studies. As a result, whether or not school choice is effective depends on one's viewpoint instead of on research-based evidence. The following summary of available information about outcomes of school choice focuses on areas of student achievement and parental satisfaction.

School choice has not, in most cases, led to marked improvement in test scores. Comprehensive studies of available data from Milwaukee and Cleveland voucher programs raise as many questions about the academic benefits to students as they give conclusive answers (U.S. General Accounting Office, 2001). The U.S. General Accounting Office report looked at findings across studies of student performance. To ensure high standards of data quality, the authors of the report included only research that used either an experimental or a quasi-experimental design, had large sample sizes, and had relatively high response rates. From these studies, very few data support the premise that school choice leads to stronger student performance. Much of the discussion in this area surrounds the need for controlled, experimental studies with sufficient data across school years. It is only in this way that we can come to understand the sustained impact of school choice on student achievement.

Inconclusive evidence for vouchers parallels similar reports that, on average, private education also does not necessarily increase student outcomes (Braun, Jenkins, & Grigg, 2006; U.S. General Accounting Office, 2001). Studies of student success in private versus public schools usually rely on standardized test scores such as the National Assessment of Educational Progress (NAEP) or a state-administered assessment. The National Center for Education Statistics analyzed NAEP reading and math scores for fourth and eighth graders in both private and public schools (Braun, Jenkins, & Grigg, 2006). Their analysis showed that students in private schools did not perform demonstrably higher than those in public schools when student characteristics were taken into account. Student characteristics included in this analysis were gender, race, disability status, socioeconomic status, and English Language Learner status. *It was these student characteristics, and not the school characteristics* (private vs. public, teacher experience, school size, etc.), that had the greatest impact on student achievement. Although subsequent analysis of the data confirms some results and questions others, these findings go against the assumption that private schools give students a substantial academic edge over public schools.

The driving force behind use of school choice will be parental satisfaction with their neighborhood schools (Howell, 2004). If parents are, on the whole, pleased with their local resources, it is unlikely that they will elect to go to other schools that may be further away. Recent research shows that parents are actually far more satisfied with the quality of their local schools than in previous years. This finding comes perhaps as a surprise in light of the attention paid to the growing number of schools that are labeled "in need of improvement" under NCLB. Parents appear to be quite forgiving in terms of student test scores as long as teachers and staff members are caring and responsive to their needs. They may also see value in what the school brings to their families and communities beyond what is measured in a single standardized test. The one issue that parents are quick to criticize is school safety (Hochschild, 2003); accountability reforms have laid some groundwork for addressing this concern but will need greater emphasis to have an impact on student safety.

School Choice and Students Who Are Deaf or Hard of Hearing

There are several assumptions behind the discussions surrounding school choice; the extent to which they apply to students who are deaf or hard of hearing varies greatly, depending on the assumption. For students who are deaf or hard of hearing, issues of public school choice intersect with issues of placement that are a part of determining services. The criteria for determining student placement, under IDEA, is based on student needs and district resources, not accountability to parents for student achievement. Under IDEA, parents, teachers, and administrators work on a case-by-case basis to determine what placement would be the least restrictive environment (LRE) for students with disabilities. As a result of how the LRE clause has been implemented, there has been a significant shift toward including students with disabilities in regular education settings (discussed in Chapter 1). On the one hand, this trend in implementing LRE means that students who are deaf or hard of hearing have access to school choice policies more than in the past when they were more likely to be enrolled in a separate education setting. On the other hand, for students who are deaf or hard of hearing receiving services under IDEA, the match between student needs and educational setting resources continues to drive school enrollment decisions, not accountability reforms.

The first assumption behind accountability-based school choice is that parents who use school choice options are more invested in their child's education and, thus, demonstrate increased involvement in school activities. Parent involvement is seen as a critical component of student success, one that is lacking in many struggling schools. Common indicators of parental involvement include whether they attend parent-teacher conferences and/or large meetings or participate as a volunteer in classroom activities. The assumption is that student achievement will increase if parents are involved in the education process; school choice may be one way to engage parents in their children's education. In reality, although parent involvement has been demonstrated to predict student academic achievement, it does not seem to be a significant factor in parents' use of school choice options (Calderon, 2000).

Choice for students who are deaf or hard of hearing is even more complex than for students without disabilities. Students who are deaf or hard of hearing are among those students who have been most underserved and yet also rely on a greater number of professional staff members with specialized training. Parents of students with IEPs, including students who are deaf or hard of hearing, are already involved in the educational placement details of their child's education. What is most important to parents of students who are deaf or hard of hearing is whether their children receive the kind of services they need, for example, an educational interpreter in regular education settings or the option to attend a regional program for students who are deaf or hard of hearing. Parent involvement may need to be increased for students who are deaf or hard of hearing, but school choice is unlikely to be the mechanism to do so unless a school's ability to provide needed services is a part of eligibility for a school choice option.

For example, suppose a Deaf student is enrolled in a mainstream setting with an educational interpreter. The student's right to a free and appropriate public education has been met, but the educational interpreter may be only of adequate quality and the student's achievement may not be up to his potential. Under IDEA, the parents may not have the leverage needed to raise the quality of the interpreter services. Suppose further that a neighboring school or district is host to an educational interpreter training program where the student could have access to higher quality interpreting services. IDEA may not allow for parents to request a transfer to the new school, but a school choice option based on accountability for quality of services and educational outcomes may provide greater flexibility for parents in making a switch.

A second assumption is that school choice will result in a "pseudo-free-market education" economy (Hess & Finn, 2004). In a free-market economy, different groups compete for consumers, thus encouraging businesses to improve the quality of their product and to reduce costs. School choice advocates say that without school choice, districts have a relative monopoly on education, and schools have little external incentive to improve (Colvin, 2004). Under public school financing structures, funds for students go to the schools they attend (Plank & Dunbar, 2004). In traditional enrollment policies, parents have little fiscal impact on a school. Under school choice, if students move to another school, the monies also go with them, allowing parents to "vote with their feet." Using the economics metaphor, parents who are dissatisfied with the quality of their neighborhood school (or product) can choose a different, competing school. Under this rationale, those schools with a quality product will survive and those with poor results will be forced to close or reorganize due to insufficient enrollment. If there is enough capacity available in "good" schools, then it is feasible that there would be an exodus from the schools that do not produce high student outcomes.

Among the rationales for why accountability-based school choice policies are effective, the pseudo-free-market assumption actually holds the strongest promise for students who are deaf or hard of hearing. Students who are deaf or hard of hearing represent tuition dollars for the chosen school, particularly if the fair cost of their education (i.e., cost of accommodations, tutoring, or interpreters) is included in funding allocations. The first condition that needs to be met is for more than one school or district to be "competing" for students who are deaf or hard of hearing. For choice to make sense, a parent of a student who is deaf or hard of hearing must have options to choose between. Each of these options would need to be able to provide the services required under IDEA. A second condition is that schools or programs report sufficient information about student performance, teacher quality, and as indicated above, school safety. Parents would need to have enough information about school effectiveness to make a sound decision about the match for their child. A third condition is that students could be reasonably transported to the school option; many students who are deaf or hard of hearing already travel great distances to attend schools for the deaf or regional programs. Combining school choice with student placement decisions may therefore be most relevant in high-density areas such as large urban school districts. In summary, with appropriate reports of school or program data, parents could choose between at least two viable options for their students who are deaf or hard of hearing.

Accountability reforms play a role in legal disputes over educational placement of students who are deaf or hard of hearing. Placement decisions can sometimes be contested, with parents seeking one option (such as a school for the deaf) and a district claiming that the local option fulfills their obligations under IDEA. Because enrollment at a school for the deaf is more expensive than enrollment in the regular education setting, cost becomes a factor in how such decisions are made. In a legal dispute, accountability-based choice could become a part of the discussion as to the effectiveness of school services for students who are deaf or hard of hearing. For example, if School A has a high accountability-based ranking, particularly for students who are deaf or hard of hearing, it may be seen as a more appropriate placement than School B with an insufficient success rating. Accountability measures of student performance would therefore provide (a) information that was previously missing from placement decisions for students who are deaf or hard of hearing and (b) grounds for parents to ask that accountability data be included in the free and appropriate public education comparison between two options.

The last assumption behind school choice is about the quality of public versus private education. Many of the school choice programs (e.g., Milwaukee) provide vouchers to parents to send their children to private schools. The premise that private education is better than public education does not apply to students who are deaf or hard of hearing in the same way it might apply to students without hearing loss. For students under IDEA, *ability to pay does not play a large role in whether or not a child attends a private school*. If the local school or district is not able to provide a free and appropriate public education and if the parents can successfully argue that a free and appropriate public education would best be provided by a private school, then the district must pay those tuition costs. The income level of families of students who are deaf or hard of hearing in private schools may thus be, on average, lower than the rest of the student body. The reality is, however, that most private and parochial schools do not have the staff members to accommodate students with disabilities. Yet there are special cases when private schools provide needed resources for students who are deaf or hard of hearing. For example, there are some states without a public school for the deaf. A student's needs may be best served by a *private* school for the deaf. In this situation, IDEA would allow for district funds to be provided for the student to attend the private school. The quality of the regular education school is evaluated based on its ability to serve the *individual* students who are deaf or hard of hearing, not on overall measures of student achievement on the state assessment. Once again, it is the educational placement decision, and not the accountability reform, that guides the school choice decision for students who are deaf or hard of hearing.

Targeted Choice Programs

General models of school choice are unlikely to guarantee the kind of specific instruction and resources provided under IDEA. In this sense, NCLB and similar accountability reforms are not inclusive in their school choice models.

Within accountability, school choice does not focus on the individual needs of the child but on the overall performance of schools. Choice programs designed specifically for students with disabilities may be most appropriate when looking at options for students who are deaf or hard of hearing, particularly those who otherwise enroll in regular education settings.

As part of a growing concern that parents of children with disabilities need more options, Florida has initiated a large-scale program to provide school choice specifically to parents of students with disabilities (Florida Department of Education, n.d.). The McKay Scholarship Program in Florida allows students to transfer either to another public school or to a private school in a voucher program. These vouchers extend to residential or medical care facilities for students with severe needs or complex medical conditions. The amount of the voucher is equal to either the tuition charged by the receiving institution or the amount that the state spends to serve a student with that particular disability. The demand for access to this program has been phenomenal. A total of nearly 16,000 students participated in the McKay Scholarship Program in the 2004–05 school year, an increase of nearly 7,000 from 2002–03. Other initiatives are also under way in Arizona, Georgia, Utah, and Ohio (Alliance for School Choice, n.d.).

Although outcome measures for students have not yet been reported, parents clearly want to take advantage of a voucher option specifically designed for students with disabilities. For many students, private schools with resources specifically designed to meet the needs of students with disabilities may be an improvement over public schools without full-time specialists in that area. Gaining access to specialized private education can be challenging under IDEA, especially when the student is receiving an adequate free and appropriate public education. Yet private programs may be able to offer a more individualized educational environment for students with special needs. By extension, targeted special education vouchers may be a viable option for students who are deaf or hard of hearing, particularly if they have multiple disabilities and would benefit from schools that specialize in meeting their needs.

Potential Obstacles to School Choice

The goal of accountability-based school choice is to provide a stronger consequence to districts and schools for inadequate student achievement. There are, however, some key limiting factors to the implementation of school choice under NCLB (Colvin, 2004). Four limitations (district capacity, funding for transportation, notification process, and schools as communities) are discussed below.

The first limiting factor to school choice is district capacity. For school choice to be an option, districts must have excess space in performing schools for students who want to transfer from underperforming schools (Sanchez, 2006). In some cases, higher performing schools simply do not have enough seats. For example, in 2007, the Los Angeles Unified School District was 160,000 seats short of where it needs to be to accommodate the district transfers (Sanchez, 2006). The district has a substantial building plan under way, with 160 new schools in the works, but it will take years, if not a decade, to complete. Parents who are unable to transfer their children to a successful school may have to wait until the construction program is finished. For those students who are deaf or hard of hearing in regular education who might want to transfer to another regular school within the district, limited capacity adds yet another constraint onto an already complicated picture of accountability-based school choice. In contrast, schools for the deaf are not limited in their capacities due to decreases in enrollment over the past several years. Accountability-based school choice decisions that result in enrollment at schools for the deaf may not face the same capacity issues found in regular education.

A related limitation is that some districts may not have a school that has met AYP. This limitation applies mainly to students who are deaf or hard of hearing in regular education, either in an inclusive setting or in a district program for students who are deaf or hard of hearing. AYP limitations occur when all schools in the district have been designated as underperforming or where a district does not have more than one school serving each grade range. For example, rural districts that have only one high school cannot offer an alternative to parents if that one school has not met AYP. In this case, districts are to have options in another school district. In rural communities especially, the school choice option is often a significant distance from the failing school. School choice is therefore primarily an option for families that live in districts with multiple schools with a range of performance levels, for example, AYP, not AYP, or Safe Harbor (Howell, 2004; Medler, 2004). As time goes on and benchmarks increase, more and more schools are projected to fall into "underperforming" categories. The number of districts with schools that have met AYP will therefore diminish, as will choice options for parents of students who are deaf or hard of hearing in underperforming schools.

The second limiting factor to accountability-based school choice is limited funds for transportation. Although districts are to use a portion of their Title I funds to bus students to the new school, there is a cap on how much they are required to spend. In some districts, the demand may outpace the available funds for transportation to a chosen school. Parents who have students at underperforming schools but who cannot afford to take them to the new school themselves may find that choice options are much narrower than if transportation were guaranteed for all students. If allocations are sufficient, however, this school choice provision could be advantageous to students who are deaf or hard of hearing. Students who are deaf or hard of hearing who attend regional programs or schools for the deaf, particularly if they enroll out of their own initiative and not as part of an IDEA IEP decision process, pay for their own transportation to school. If a student who is deaf or hard of hearing and who qualifies for Title I funding transfers to a different school due to accountability-based school choice, then additional funding for transportation may be available that would not otherwise have been in place.

The third limiting factor to school choice use is the notification process. Districts are responsible for notifying parents as to their eligibility for school choice under accountability reform. However, there have been examples of delays in notifying parents such that it becomes very difficult to transfer after the start of the school year (Maranto & Maranto, 2004). Sometimes these delays are not a result of the district's negligence, however. Districts are often in a bind because test companies have been delayed in their reports of student assessment scores (Cole, 2006). It takes time to compile school report cards of AYP and to ensure that there are not errors in those reports. As a result, parents are often left in the dark as to the status of their school and whether school choice will be available to them in the upcoming school year (Hannaway, 2004). In 2004, 20 states did not provide the schools with their AYP status until after the start of the next school year (Stullich, Eisner, McCrary & Roney, 2006). Parents of students who are deaf or hard of hearing in educational settings that serve students from multiple referring districts (e.g., schools for the deaf and regional programs for students who are deaf or hard of hearing), face even greater obstacles in obtaining correct information about school choice eligibility. Building capacity at the state and district level to process assessment results and make AYP designations will be an important part of improving accountability-based school choice in future years.

Finally, there are social factors at play in the success of accountability-based school choice. Schools are not just places to consume knowledge; they are social institutions that are a part of the community. School teams, family history, and neighborhood social relationships are all integral to the fabric of school life (Maranto & Maranto, 2004). Moving to a different school is not only a matter of concerns about student scores on assessments but also a question of how to maintain involvement in community life. The neighborhood school system is part of the glue that holds a community together through teachers who live in the area, sports teams, and school events. Parents are usually reluctant to remove their children from that support network that integrates both home and community resources. Additional expenses and logistical issues involving transportation, ability to participate in extracurricular activities, and continuity between home and school peers all contribute to the desire to stay at the neighborhood school.

For students who are deaf or hard of hearing, particularly those who are Deaf and from Deaf families, schools as communities take on additional meaning. Schools for the deaf are often a hub of social and cultural interaction for the Deaf community. Alumni strongly identify with their school when they graduate and go into the workplace. Schools for the deaf also serve as a place where American Sign Language is used by a large group of individuals in an academic, but also social, setting. Residential schools, where students also spend time outside of the school day, play a particularly strong role in developing and maintaining a cultural Deaf identity. The sense of community may encourage parents of students who are deaf or hard of hearing in regular education schools to find ways to attend schools for the deaf, but school choice options for students to *leave* schools for the deaf, given the strong community element, are unlikely to motivate many parents.

Given the above factors, it is perhaps not surprising that most eligible students do not exercise their NCLB school choice option. In 2003–04, 3.9 million students nationwide were eligible for school choice (Stullich et al., 2006). However, only 38,000 students used their choice option, less than 1% of all those who were eligible for school transfers (Stullich et al., 2006). This figure rose slightly in 2004–05 to 45,000 students (Stullich et al., 2006). State and district choice policies are sometimes more lenient than those offered under NCLB (Colvin, 2004). The number of students using transportation services supported by NCLB funds is one of the only ways to track these changes when districts have multiple transfer and school choice enrollment options (Medler, 2004). In some districts, it is not possible to tell whether students transfer due to accountability options or due to preexisting transfer policies. Accountability-based school choice has not, thus far, had a significant impact on parents' decisions on where to send their children to school.

Recommendations for Action

School choice, as conceptualized under NCLB, appears to have a minimal impact on students who are deaf or hard of hearing. IDEA is the driving force behind educational placement, not accountability reform. There is potential good in school choice policies, though, particularly if combined with an improved assessment and evaluation system as recommended in previous chapters. The following recommendations for action therefore draw from the discussion in this chapter and presume that a strong accountability framework is also in place.

The first policy recommendation relates to the School Safety option provided under NCLB. The current model allows each state to define what is meant by "persistently dangerous" and then requires the school administrators to collect and report information to make that determination. Although state control over content area standards and proficiency cutoffs has roots in the history of education administration in the United States, extending this local control to safety standards is, in my mind, detrimental to the purpose of accountability. This policy can be improved in two ways. First, a national standard for safety can be implemented after a review of current state policies and a discussion of what truly constitutes a dangerous school. Parent and student input on school safety is an excellent element to include in a comprehensive evaluation framework. Second, the criterion for persistently dangerous should be defined in a way that allows for an external check on supporting data. For example, if parents are surveyed about the violence level at a school, the survey should be conducted and summarized by an external party, not the school itself. These findings should also be made public along with reports of student performance on state assessments.

A second recommendation is part policy, part practice. As noted in the chapter, notification of school choice options is essential for the implementation of this component of accountability reform. Schools and districts are often overloaded with administrative tasks related to accountability reform. For parents of students who are deaf or hard of hearing at a school for the deaf or regional program that does not have its own school report card, eligibility for school choice is based on each individual family's place of residence (see Chapter 5 for further detail on school report cards). With the exception of schools for the deaf and regular education schools that have their own accountability report card, dissemination of this information does not make sense at the school or program level. It may be best to establish a school choice information dissemination branch at the state level. This approach would streamline the process of (a) obtaining school eligibility information, (b) identifying school choice options within and outside the district, (c) identifying Title I families, and (d) notifying families directly about their options. Options would need to be tailored for students who are deaf or hard of hearing to incorporate the student placement options under IDEA. This centralization would come with drawbacks, including a lack of knowledge about the families the schools serve and the challenge of providing usable guidelines about accountability school choices and IDEA placement decisions. However, state-level notification would also increase the chance of a consistent notification rate for all families in the state. The state director of services for students who are deaf or hard of hearing could also be involved in assisting families who are eligible for accountability school choice. This process would be applicable for school choice eligibility based on student achievement measures and on school safety ratings.

The first research task is to be able to *describe* the level of school choice that occurs for students who are deaf or hard of hearing. Tracking school choice among families with students who are deaf or hard of hearing requires more integrated data collection systems than are currently available. For example, school choice decisions under NCLB are difficult to monitor due to conflicts with a variety of local policies that are already in place (Medler, 2004). Disaggregating public school choice transfers by disability status, or by whether or not students are deaf or hard of hearing, will be a further challenge. It is likely that early reports of public school choice for students who are deaf or hard of hearing will therefore be from the local level, stemming first from family advocacy groups and organizations that help parents gain access to services or know their rights under IDEA or NCLB.

The second research task is to *understand* reasons why parents do or do not use school choice and what impact those decisions have on academic outcomes for students who are deaf or hard of hearing. A full picture of how school choice affects students who are deaf or hard of hearing will require broad participation by parents and families in districts that offer public school choice. This effort is really where we will best capture the impact of school choice availability on students who are deaf or hard of hearing. For example, parents who have accountability-based school choice options can provide insights on the process and whether it helped them leverage more choices for their child. Did their district programs let them know whether their school of residence was required to notify parents as to its AYP status? For students who used interpreters or other educational aides, were the same or appropriate resources available to students if they transferred to a new school? Outcomes are equally important to measure, including student performance on accountability measures and parent satisfaction with the school choice results. This kind of dialogue about the implications of accountability-based school choice, both positive and negative, will be an important way for parents to help inform future education policy development.

One of the greatest challenges in implementing accountability-based school choice has been the actual step of informing parents of their options in a timely manner. The first practice recommendation therefore applies to administrators who work with parents of students who are deaf or hard of hearing, whether they be school or district level staff members. Because placement decisions for students who are deaf or hard of hearing, at least those under IDEA, do not typically include issues of accountability choice, options under these stipulations may be excluded from school enrollment decisions. This circumstance is true not only for student achievement measures but also for school safety concerns. Whether this information dissemination occurs as part of the IEP plan development process or as a general notification to parents would depend on the school context. For example, administrators at regular education schools may want to clarify what implications there are for students who are referred to or from a school with an "in need of improvement" rating that triggers a school choice option for parents. The goal here is to bring relevant school choice elements into the ongoing conversation about placement decisions for students who are deaf or hard of hearing.

The second two practice recommendations apply, as is fitting for this chapter, to parents. First, parents may be able to use public school choice opportunities to choose a school that has greater curricular or extracurricular resources to serve their deaf or hard of hearing child. IDEA guarantees a free and appropriate public education, but ensuring that educational resources are excellent, not just adequate, is not enforced under this law. IDEA certainly does not measure levels of student proficiency in the manner outlined by NCLB. Specific to students who are deaf or hard of hearing, there are likely to be differences at a local level in the skill of teachers who work with students on key areas such as communication or development of literacy skills. Supporting staff members such as higher quality interpreters or speech specialists may be available at another school in the district. Individual teachers or schools may be more open to a collaborative IEP development process that includes the parent and student perspective. Because resources for low-incidence disabilities can be scarce, parents may use accountability-based school choice as an opportunity to transfer to schools with more direct experience teaching students who are deaf or hard of hearing—an option that may not be available under IDEA alone.

Second, working in conjunction with other parents, families may cooperate to create a cluster of students with hearing loss in the school of their choice. In a district without a set program for students who are deaf or hard of hearing, parents may be able to use choice to provide similar peers for their children. Families across a district (if all are at schools where they are eligible for school choice) may also use accountability reform to leverage district resources for more comprehensive support services for their children. Finally, parents who are dissatisfied with school safety issues can "vote with their feet" and use accountability-based choice as a further resource in transferring their child to a more desirable school.

Conclusion

School choice reforms taps into two deeply held American ideals: first, that all students should have access to a free, safe, quality education and, second, that a free market will result in competition between schools and, thus, in better education. In reality, these principles pull against each other, and as a result, neither of these ideals conforms exactly to the needs of public education in the United States. Furthermore, the advantages or disadvantages of school choice are potentially different depending on a student's characteristics. For students who may benefit from specialized instruction, or even just more intensive instruction, finding a school that is a good fit with student needs can be the difference between a sufficient education and a poor one. In other words, the stakes are high, and perhaps higher for students with special needs. Parents of students who are deaf or hard of hearing often face hugely challenging decisions about identifying school placement, obtaining services, and providing their child with the support he or she needs to succeed. Navigating the potential resources offered by accountability reforms, for example, a school transfer or additional tutoring, is layered on top of what is already a very complex process.

8

Accountability and Students Who Are Deaf or Hard of Hearing

Chapter 8 marks the closure of this book with a discussion of how public education can be accountable to students who are deaf or hard of hearing. Accountability reform language tends to focus on who is being *held* accountable, either individuals or institutions. But what is it we are being held accountable *for*? And to *whom*? These additional questions assume a perspective that is both goal oriented (e.g., to raise student outcomes) and people specific (e.g., schools accountable to parents for student outcomes). The current accountability reforms focus on the schools and districts as the agent of change instead of the students, teachers, and parents as participants in improving education. For example, throughout this book we have seen examples of how current accountability reforms define school "success." Schools are successful (or at least not failing) if they have enough students reach proficiency benchmarks on state assessments. Schools are successful if their teachers all have required teaching credentials. Schools are successful if they do not have high levels of reported violence, and so on. But the activities of teaching and learning and the routes to student success are far more complex than these indicators allow. As a result, the external measures of accountability reform provide a picture of success that, while at times is informative, does not capture what we know truly leads to high-quality education.

If the structure of accountability reform is cursory in how it defines, measures, and facilitates quality education for the overall student population, it is even more so in its considerations for students who are deaf or hard of hearing. Accountability reform, as it is currently conceptualized, cannot bring the kind of change it seeks. In most cases, policy is inconsistent in how it includes students who are deaf or hard of hearing and the educational structures that serve them. One of the great challenges of school reform is to make that reform flexible enough to be meaningful for students with diverse backgrounds and educational needs. For students who are deaf or hard of hearing, accountability reform raises additional, equally important questions about their education. Many of these questions were salient long before NCLB and will remain so for future versions of accountability reforms. The remainder of this chapter summarizes issues raised across different sections of this book. In this discussion, I include recommendations for an accountability structure that might better facilitate improved learning outcomes for students who are deaf or hard of hearing.

Deaf Education and Measures of Success

This book began with an exploration of the deaf education context and aspects that may interact with the current accountability reform approach. Accountability reforms initially gained ground because of the belief that public education does not produce adequately prepared students. Does this assumption apply to deaf education? Although there are strengths in instructional strategies for students who are deaf or hard of hearing, there certainly have been struggles, particularly in reading. This steep learning curve is due to many factors related to the need for early exposure to language and the problems inherent in "cracking the code" of written English. Although many students do make progress in reading and in other academic areas, many students who are deaf or hard of hearing graduate from high school without grade-level knowledge and skills.

Under NCLB, the AYP report cards are steadily becoming a showcase for how to report school failures, not school successes or even progress toward reasonable goals. One recommendation is to extend the time line for progress beyond 2014, or perhaps even remove a time frame all together. The fact that this rate of progress is greater than what has been accomplished by even the most successful school or by the most comprehensive school reforms calls the feasibility of this goal into question (Linn, 2005a, 2005b). Although reducing the achievement gap is a commendable goal, bringing every student to proficiency in such a short time frame, without any real change in instruction, seems to be an unreasonable expectation (Linn, 2003a; McCombs, Kirby, Barney, Darilek, & Magee, 2004). Schools for the deaf would benefit from this extended time line because students who are deaf or hard of hearing often arrive at school below grade level in language, beginning reading skills, and other academic skills. Although progress can continually be made as a cohort moves through the system, unless new students arrive with more solid language and academic skills, schools cannot make up that experience for individual students except over time. In other words, when a school's new students need more than a year to meet grade-level standards, the school as a whole will never meet 100% proficiency.

Claims about the failing status of deaf education are misleading in several ways. One of the difficulties in using accountability reform to evaluate deaf education is the limited number of educational settings that are explicitly included in the accountability reforms. Right now, the basis for evaluating deaf education relies on only a handful of schools for the deaf and on the few states that report student achievement by disability status. Educational settings for students who are deaf or hard of hearing are far more diverse than what is represented by data-reporting structures under NCLB. Because of the great shift in enrollment from specialized programs to inclusive education settings, "deaf education" as a single concept may not exist. On the one hand, students in a school for the deaf are likely to experience deaf education with the potential for different language use in instruction, Deaf culture, and strategies developed by specialists in the field. On the other hand, students in regular education settings can go through their school careers without a deaf peer or a teacher of the deaf. The "deaf" in deaf education, in this case, refers to the *student* more than the pedagogical context. Current accountability reforms focus almost solely on the context, or the school that a student attends. This point is just one example of how the structure of accountability is not a good fit for students who are deaf or hard of hearing.

The impact of accountability on deaf education thus depends almost entirely on the circumstance of the individual student. This reality is in tension with the current focus on the school setting as the agent of change. A recommended component for a future accountability model is to report student performance across settings, particularly for low-incidence groups such as students who are deaf or hard of hearing. Again, the focus here shifts from the institution, as it were, of "deaf education" to the educational outcomes of students who are deaf or hard of hearing as a group. This perspective may diffuse the responsibility of schools for student outcomes, but it does move the emphasis to the population of students who are deaf or hard of hearing that is served by deaf education *across* settings. This recommended emphasis on aggregating and reporting data based on *student* characteristics, and not (only) *school* characteristics, provides a clearer picture of how accountability reforms affect students from low-incidence groups. In conjunction with recommendations for better measurement and reporting mechanisms (Chapters 4 and 5), this shift will help educators and policymakers use assessment information to its full potential.

Access to the Curriculum

Before students can perform well on assessments, they must have exposure to test content and quality instruction. Even though the specific standards supporting the "opportunity to learn" are not required as part of NCLB, ensuring this opportunity can be a conceptual driving force behind measurement and eventual reform efforts (Guiton & Oakes, 1995; Herman, Klein, & Abedi, 2000). The goal of reforms focused on the opportunity to learn is to determine whether students have received adequate instruction to be expected to perform on accountability assessments. Top-down reforms, focused on having policy and standards lead teaching and learning in educational change, should lead to more scrutiny of classroom-level activities. The third recommendation for a more responsive accountability framework is to include some measure of the content area standards related to the opportunity to learn.

When thinking about what access students who are deaf or hard of hearing have to standards-based curriculum, important issues arise, including teacher knowledge of core content area, robust communication skills for both students and teachers, and appropriate accommodations to actively participate in classroom learning. Measuring opportunity to learn can capture the extent to which the classroom environment (e.g., quality of educational interpreting) is conducive to grade-level learning for students who are deaf or hard of hearing.

In summary, instruction is a key element missing from the current accountability measures. Both increasing instructional time and continuing to raise the level of coursework are implied, but not explicit, components of NCLB. Instead, the standards, assessment, and consequences components are assumed to create a climate where instruction and learning improve. There is little research that supports this assumption (Hess & Finn, 2004). We do not understand the direct and indirect factors that leverage this kind of change. Although the purpose of accountability is to close the achievement gap, there is little information about *how* the actions taken under this accountability framework will actually bring about this change (Tough, 2006). The approaches taken to provide instruction may vary widely for different student populations, but accurately ascertaining what students learn is essential to measuring the effects of education.

Challenges in Testing and Measurement

Chapters 4 and 5 gave an analysis of the assessment and reporting components of accountability reforms. Testing accommodations play a critical role in increasing access to the content of state standardized assessments for students who are deaf or hard of hearing. There are a great number of concerns regarding the implementation of accommodations for high-stakes tests. Issues that most apply to students who are deaf or hard of hearing are (a) what is measured on the tests, (b) the validity of the test scores when tests are taken with accommodations, and (c) the limited number of states that allow alternate assessment formats for students who are deaf or hard of hearing. Each of these issues is critical to address in a revised accountability model that is responsive to the needs of students who are deaf or hard of hearing.

When looking at how accountability reform uses "in need of improvement" school designations, a first consideration is to be clear about what is and what is not measured in the state assessments. Students in schools for the deaf make strides (as do all students) in many more areas than are reflected by scores on standardized assessments. The education community, including the Deaf community, has expressed frustration with respect to the limited information about student growth available on standardized assessments. An improved approach to measurement in accountability will emphasize the use of multiple measures of student knowledge and skill. In the context of assessment currently used by states, this improved approach may broaden the use of alternate assessments or even targeted portfolios to demonstrate student achievement over the school year. In an expanded view, measures of student success might include individual goals such as progress toward IEP goals (for those students with an IEP). Models for this kind of approach have been found within the deaf education community, most specifically at South Carolina School for the Deaf (Cawthon, 2008).

The second concern for those involved in assessment policy is the validity of assessments taken with different accommodations. Although accommodations such as extended time and small groups are not controversial and are allowed in most states, other types of accommodations require more research before policies can be consistent from state to state. Research that investigates the validity of assessments with interpreters for students who are deaf or hard of hearing will be important future work. The perspectives of educators of students who are deaf or hard of hearing are also important when looking at differential effects of accommodations for students with different language and academic backgrounds. Including all affected parties in these considerations can contribute to building a stronger knowledge base on the validity of accommodations used in standardized assessment.

Another key recommendation for an improved accountability framework is to allow for greater local input about the effects of using accommodations. Something that is typically missing from the study of accommodations use is reflection on how well the process went for an individual student, not only in terms of logistics but also in terms of its purpose—to increase access to test content. Discussions between students, parents, and teachers to evaluate the effectiveness of the accommodation would be a beneficial component of how we understand the assessment process. It is also possible to directly measure the effectiveness of assessment accommodations; research in this vein is currently under way. Formal use of tools that take multiple factors into account will be particularly relevant for students who are deaf or hard of hearing.

Alternate assessments are a growing area of research and discussion when considering accountability, tests of student proficiency, and students with disabilities. There are several issues for those students taking alternate assessments that parallel issues for those students who participate in standardized assessments using testing accommodations. For example, test scores for students who take alternate assessments may not be counted as "proficient" when included in the overall accountability framework. Similarly, scores for tests that are taken with accommodations are viewed as invalidating scores for tests that were taken without the accommodation when both sets of scores are aggregated. Therefore, important questions arise about skills and knowledge measured by alternate assessments and whether students who use these assessments are able to demonstrate proficiency on state standards (for the purpose of accountability).

Although there is strong support in the field for the use of alternate assessments for students who do not have the English Language proficiency or the academic preparation for a grade-level standardized assessment, current accountability policy discourages the use of an alternate assessment with all but very severely disabled students. Usually, students who are deaf or hard of hearing are not included in that category unless they have multiple disabilities, particularly physical and cognitive disabilities. Nevertheless, the number of students who are deaf or hard of hearing who do actually participate in an alternate assessment is usually above and beyond the maximum percentage of students who can participate and have their scores counted toward AYP (Cawthon, 2007). An additional recommendation is to allow for greater flexibility in the use of alternate assessments. Limitations that are based on relative frequency do not honor the purpose of alternate assessments. In other words, decisions regarding one student's use of an alternate assessment should not impinge on whether or not another student also receives this format due to caps on its use at a single school site.

Teacher Preparation

At the heart of accountability and teacher-quality reform is the assumption that stronger teacher certification standards will result in better teachers. But, as Ding and Sherman (2006) point out, it can be difficult to tease out the teacher effects (characteristics such as years of experience or type of certification) and teacher effectiveness. *Teacher effectiveness* is reflected by how well students learn from the instructional strategies and classroom activities that are led by the teacher or teaching team. The next recommendation for a more flexible accountability reform is to include teacher effectiveness characteristics in an evaluation of teacher quality. Furthermore, these characteristics could include those needed to teach the students they serve, in particular, students who are deaf or hard of hearing. There is a great deal of variation in individual student characteristics and how they interact with teacher characteristics. Looking only at certification level or content area knowledge does not allow for an understanding of student outcomes that are a result of interaction between student, family, community, and teacher, and classroom. Accountability reforms do not currently measure the specific effectiveness a teacher's instruction has on student achievement while controlling for the many other factors that are involved in how a student learns. Even if the accountability reforms do not measure effectiveness in this way, the deaf education community needs these kinds of studies.

A second theme from the review of quality teacher preparation programs is one of partnerships: partnerships with schools, partnering between teacher preparation faculty, and partnerships between schools and families. Accountability reforms need to include support for partnerships as a way to facilitate improved student outcomes. These partnerships are especially important for teachers who work with low-incidence disability groups such as students who are deaf or hard of hearing. Johnson (2003b) asserts that improving teacher preparation will require a focus on (a) gaining a "critical mass," or sufficient numbers of individuals in a shared learning space, and (b) encouraging learning contexts where both students and teachers work collaboratively in constructivist learning activities. Technology tools such as Join Together Project is one way that teachers can create a virtual community across time and space. Continued dialogue and partnerships for teachers working in schools for the deaf, regional programs, and mainstreamed settings will be essential in continuing the professional development opportunities teachers need.

A third theme is continued support after teachers are placed in the field. Schools, districts, and teacher preparation programs that participate in partnerships and dialogue with teachers can leverage the kinds of resources that are known to reduce attrition for teachers, particularly those in challenging educational settings. Accountability reforms might consider measuring retention rates, which could add to measures of school success and could provide support for induction programs if needed. Administrators will want to keep in mind factors that are important to special education teacher retention—responsive induction programs, deliberate role design, positive work conditions and supports, and professional development. These retention-enhancing factors also serve to cultivate qualified special educators by providing the conditions in which they can thrive and grow professionally.

Parent Involvement

Parents' involvement in their child's education is one of the most important factors in a child's academic success. Parents of students who are deaf or hard of hearing are encouraged to become engaged in the educational process through dialogue with teachers, both informally and through formal IEP team discussions. Yet many parents do not have the information they need to fully advocate for their children's needs. Current accountability reform has heightened the high-stakes nature of education by holding schools accountable for the learning outcomes of all students. The law also brings a new option to engage parents in their child's education, options that may not have been present before: school choice.

The implications of the school choice option for students who receive special services in the schools are still unclear. If school choice is included in future accountability reforms, then policies should clarify how these choices interact with educational placement decisions for students with disabilities. Parents of students who are deaf or hard of hearing potentially have the legal right to resources and services under both NCLB and IDEA. It is possible that school choice might be used as leverage if parents wish to transfer to a school for the deaf and had previously been unable to demonstrate to the district that this option would be a stronger one for their child.

Another place for awareness is how the state measures school safety and how that information is communicated to parents. Safety is an issue that schools and districts must communicate about clearly to parents. Parents can be a part of the effort to push local leaders to provide public documentation of safety levels. If the state definition of "persistently dangerous" is vague or allows for a high percentage of incidents per student, work could also be done to revise these definitions to allow for action sooner rather than later.

The Future of Accountability and Students Who Are Deaf or Hard of Hearing

Accountability reform, regardless of its strengths and weaknesses, has focused a great deal of attention on student outcomes. The question for those of us who serve students who are deaf or hard of hearing is how an accountability approach to education can leverage resources and strategies to benefit our students. The driving concept behind current accountability reform is that external measurement and reporting of educational outcomes will spur instructional innovation and improved student learning. Although much of the critical focus on NCLB has been on the negative consequences schools face when they do not meet AYP benchmarks, the original framework of standards, assessment, and consequences for schools can have a much more productive effect if designed to mobilize resources to improve education. In essence, there needs to be a shift in the *rationale* behind accountability reforms. For example, it can be useful to articulate curricular goals, measure student progress, and provide interventions for schools that are in need of assistance. As they currently stand, however, accountability reforms do very little to measure or change classroom practice, nor are they flexible enough to respond to the educational contexts and needs of students who are deaf or hard of hearing. Appropriately designed accountability reforms, focused on building capacity for sustained change, could actually be conceived as a diagnostic process instead of a punitive one.

Whether NCLB or another version of accountability reform, we will evaluate its worth in terms of what students can know and do after their years of schooling. Yet accountability reform makes a promise of change that it alone cannot keep. The achievement gap will not be remedied through new standards or multiple assessments; we cannot test our way out of the chronic problems of ineffective instruction, learning environments without robust communication, exclusion from content-based curriculum, standardized assessments that are not designed to give access to those with different language backgrounds, or populations that have been underserved for many years. What an accountability approach can do best is to make transparent those areas where more deliberate, formative, and constructive change can occur.

Policies and resources mobilized by an accountability reform framework, at least as it is currently designed, may best address how those changes occur.

Conclusion

There are literally thousands of parents, teachers, researchers, and policymakers who do truly want to make that positive difference for students. From each vantage point, the picture looks almost too complex to manage, and the path (or paths) to success is unclear. It can be discouraging to see how the restrictive components of NCLB resulted in even greater challenges for students who are deaf or hard of hearing than before its implementation. The realities on the ground make one wonder whether perhaps less restrictive accountability measures will be effective in motivating the systemic change that is needed to close the achievement gap. Perhaps future reauthorizations will include revisions that reflect the growing cry from the field that changes to the law need to be made. Yet, in the end, we can each do only what we have set out to do. As Helen Keller once wrote: "I am only one; but still I am one. I cannot do everything, but still I can do something." My thanks to each of you for all that you do.

References

Abernathy, S. (2007). *No Child Left Behind and the public schools.* Ann Arbor: University of Michigan Press.

Allen, T., Clark, M. D., Guidice, A., Koo, D., Lieberman, A., Mayberry, R., & Miller, P. (2009). Phonology and reading: A response to Wang, Trezek, Luckner, and Paul. *American Annals of the Deaf, 154,* 338–345.

Alliance for School Choice. (2007). School choice yearbook. Washington, DC: Author. Retrieved from http://www.allianceforschoolchoice.org/Research Resources/index.cfm?ID=2789&blnShowBack=False&idContentType=1136.

Alliance for School Choice. (n.d.). *The promise of special needs scholarships.* Washington, DC: Author. Retrieved from http://www.allianceforschoolchoice.org/ResearchResources/index.cfm?ID=2789&blnShowBack=False&idContentType=1136.

Allington, R. L., & McGill-Franzen, A. (1992). Unintended effects of educational reform in New York. *Educational Policy, 6,* 394–414.

American Association for Employment in Education (AAEE). (2003). *Educator supply and demand in the United States: 2002 research report.* Columbus, OH: Author.

American Educational Research Association (AERA), American Psychological Association (APA), & National Council on Measurement in Education (NCME). (1999). *Standards for educational and psychological testing* (3rd ed.). Washington, DC: American Educational Research Association.

Americans With Disabilities Act of 1990, Pub. L. 101-336, 42 U.S.C. § 12101.

143

Andrews, J., & Jordan, D. (1993). Minority and minority deaf professionals. *American Annals of the Deaf, 138,* 388–396.

Angrist, J., & Guryan, J. (2004, May). Teacher testing, teacher education, and teacher characteristics. *American Economic Review, 94,* 241–246.

Ansell, E., & Pagliaro, C. M. (2006). The relative difficulty of signed arithmetic story problems for primary level deaf and hard-of-hearing students. *Journal of Deaf Studies and Deaf Education, 11,* 153–170.

Antia, S., Jones, P., Reed, S., & Kreimeyer, K. (2009). Academic status and progress of deaf and hard-of-hearing students in general education classrooms. *Journal of Deaf Studies and Deaf Education, 14,* 293–311.

Asmar, M. (2006, September 17). The meaning of deafness: Parents must choose among education philosophies. *Concord Monitor,* p. 7.

August, D., & Hakuta, K. (Eds.). (1997). *Improving schooling for language-minority children: A research agenda.* Washington, DC: National Academy Press.

Barker, B., & Tomblin, B. (2004). Bimodal speech perception in infant hearing aid cochlear implant users. *Archives of Otolaryngology–Head & Neck Surgery, 130,* 582–586.

Barker, L. (2003). Computer-assisted vocabulary acquisition: The CSLU vocabulary tutor in oral-deaf education. *Journal of Deaf Studies and Deaf Education, 8,* 187–198.

Barton, P. (2006). *"Failing" or "succeeding" schools: How can we tell?* Washington, DC: American Federation of Teachers.

Bello, D. (2007, January 12). Elgin schools pull out of program for deaf. *Chicago Tribune.* Retrieved from http://www.chicagotribune.com.

Belzner, K., & Seal, B. (2009). Children with cochlear implants: A review of demographics and communication outcomes. *American Annals of the Deaf, 154,* 311–333.

Bernal, E., & Valencia, R. R. (2000). The TAAS case: A recapitulation and beyond. *Hispanic Journal of Behavioral Sciences 22,* 540–556.

Bialystok, E., Craik, F. I. M., & Ryan, J. (2006). Executive control in a modified anti-cascade task: Effects of aging and bilingualism. *Journal of Experimental Psychology: Learning Memory and Cognition, 32,* 1341–1354.

Billingsley, B. S. (2004). Special education teacher retention and attrition: A critical analysis of the research literature. *Journal of Special Education, 38,* 39–56.

Blackorby, J., & Knokey, A. (2006). *A national profile of students with hearing impairments in elementary and middle school: A special topic report from the Special Education Elementary Longitudinal Study.* Report prepared by SRI International (Project No. P10656). Washington, DC: U.S. Department of Education, Office of Special Education Programs.

Blamey, P. J., Sarant, J. Z., Paatsch, L. E., Barry, J. G., Bow, C. P., Wales, R. J., Wright, M., Psarros, C., Rattigan, K., & Tooher, R. (2001). Relationships among speech perception, production, language, hearing loss, and age in children with impaired hearing. *Journal of Speech, Language, and Hearing Research, 44,* 264–285.

Blanton, L. P., Sindelar, P. T., Correa, V. I., Hardman, M., McDonnell, J., & Kuhel, K. (2003). *Conceptions of beginning teacher quality: Models for conducting research.* Gainesville, FL: University of Florida, Center on Personnel Studies in Special Education. Retrieved from http://www.coe.ufl.edu/copsse/docs/RS-6/RS-6.pdf.

Bodner-Johnson, B. A., & Martin, D. S. (1999). Teacher educators in deaf education: Why they entered higher education and their current priorities and accomplishments. *American Annals of the Deaf, 144,* 236–241.

Boe, E. E., Barkanic, G., & Leow, C. S. (1999). *Retention and attrition of teachers at the school level: National trends and predictors.* (Data Analysis Report No. 1999-DAR1). Philadelphia: University of Pennsylvania, Graduate School of Education, Center for Research and Evaluation in Social Policy.

Boe, E. E., Bobbitt, S. A., & Cook, L. H. (1997). Whither didst thou go? Retention, reassignment, migration, and attrition of special and general education teachers from a national perspective. *Journal of Special Education, 30,* 371–389.

Bolt, S., & Thurlow, M. (2004). Five of the most frequently allowed testing accommodations in state policy: Synthesis of research. *Remedial and Special Education, 25,* 141–152.

Bowe, F. (1988). *Toward equality: Education of the deaf.* Washington, DC: Government Printing Office.

Bowen, S., & Ferrell, K. (2003). Assessment in low-incidence disabilities: The day-to-day realities. *Rural Special Education Quarterly, 22*(4), 10–16.

Bracht, N., Finnegan, J., Rissel, C., Weisbrod, R., Gleason, J., Corbett, J., & Veblen-Mortenson, S. (1994). Community ownership and program continuation following a health demonstration project. *Health Education Research, 9,* 243–255. doi: 10.1093/her/9.2.243.

Braden, J. P., & Elliott, S. N. (2003). *Accommodations on the Stanford-Binet Intelligence Scales, Fifth Edition.* (Stanford-Binet Intelligence Scales, Fifth Edition Assessment Service Bulletin No. 2). Itasca, IL: Riverside Publishing.

Brasel, K., & Quigley, S. (1977). The influence of certain language and communication environments on the development of language in deaf individuals. *Journal of Speech and Hearing Research, 20,* 95–107.

Braun, H., Jenkins, F., & Grigg, W. (2006). Comparing private schools and public schools using Hierarchical Linear Modeling. U.S. Department of Education, National Center for Education Statistics, Institute of Education Sciences (NCES No. 2006-461). Washington, DC: U.S. Government Printing Office.

Browder, D., Spooner, F., Algozzine, R., Ahlgrim-Delzell, L., Flowers, C., & Karvonen, M. (2003). What we know and need to know about alternate assessment. *Exceptional Children, 70,* 45–61.

Brown v. Board of Education of Topeka, 347 U.S. 483 (1954).

Brownell, M. T., Sindelar, P. T., Bishop, A. G., Langley, L. K., & Seo, S. (2002). Special education teacher supply and teacher quality: The problems, the solutions. *Focus on Exceptional Children, 25*(2), 1–16.

Bruce, S., DiNatale, P., & Ford, J. (2008). Meeting the needs of deaf and hard of hearing students with additional disabilities through professional teacher development. *American Annals of the Deaf, 153,* 368–375.

Calderon, R. (2000). Parent involvement in deaf children's education programs as a predictor of child's language, early reading, and social-emotional development. *Journal of Deaf Studies and Deaf Education, 5,* 140–155.

Cangiano, V. (1992). *Bilingual and ESL approaches to deaf education: Perspectives on the reading process.* Unpublished master's thesis, Hunter College, City University of New York.

Cawthon, S. (2004). Schools for the deaf and the No Child Left Behind Act. *American Annals of the Deaf, 149,* 314–323.

Cawthon, S. (2007). Hidden benefits and unintended consequences of No Child Left Behind policies for students who are deaf or hard of hearing. *American Educational Research Journal, 44,* 460–492.

Cawthon, S. (2008). No Child Left Behind and schools for the deaf: Integration into the accountability framework. In R. C. Johnson & R. Mitchell (Eds.), *Testing deaf students in an age of accountability* (pp. 92–114). Washington, DC: Gallaudet University Press.

Cawthon, S. *The future of NCLB and schools for the deaf: Change and more of the same?* Manuscript submitted for publication.

Cawthon, S., Hersh, M., Kim, S.-H., & the Online Research Lab. (2009). Accommodations for students who are deaf or hard of hearing in large-scale, standardized assessments: Surveying the landscape and charting a new direction. *Educational Measurement: Issues and Practice, 28*(2), 41–49.

Cawthon, S., & the Online Research Lab. (2006). Findings from the National Survey on Accommodations and Alternate Assessments for Students Who are Deaf or Hard of Hearing. *Journal of Deaf Studies and Deaf Education, 11,* 337–359.

Cawthon, S., & the Online Research Lab. (2007). Accommodations use for statewide standardized assessments: Prevalence and recommendations for students who are deaf or hard of hearing. *Journal of Deaf Studies and Deaf Education Advanced Access.* doi: http://dx.doi.org/10.1093/deafed/enm029.

Cawthon, S., Winton, S., Garberoglio, C., & Gobble, M. (in press). The effects of ASL as an accommodation for students who are deaf or hard of hearing. *Journal of Deaf Studies and Deaf Education.*

Cawthon, S., Wurtz, K., & the Online Research Lab. (2008). Alternate assessment use with students who are deaf or hard of hearing: An exploratory mixed methods analysis of predictors of portfolio, checklists, and out-of-level testing formats. *Journal of Deaf Studies and Deaf Education, 14,* 155–177.

The Center for the Future of Teaching and Learning. (2006). *California's teaching force: Key issues and trends.* Santa Cruz, CA: Author.

Christiansen, J., & Leigh, I. (2002). *Cochlear implants in children: Ethics and choices.* Washington, DC: Gallaudet University Press.

Clapper, A. T., Morse, A. B., Lazarus, S. S., Thompson, S. J., & Thurlow, M. L. (2005). *2003 state policies on assessment participation and accommodations for students with disabilities* (Synthesis Report No. 56). Minneapolis: University of Minnesota, National Center on Educational Outcomes. Retrieved from http://education.umn.edu/NCEO/OnlinePubs/Synthesis56.html.

Clarke, M., Haney, W., Madaus, G., Lynch, C. A., & Lynch, P. S. (2000). *High stakes testing and high school completion. Statements, 1*(3). Boston, MA: National Board on Educational Testing and Public Policy. Retrieved from http://www.bc.edu/research/nbetpp/publications/v1n3.html.

Cline, T. (1997). Education for bilingualism in different contexts: Teaching the deaf and teaching children with English as an additional language. *Educational Review, 49,* 151–158.

Cochran-Smith, M. (2001). Constructing outcomes in teacher education: Policy, practice and pitfalls. *Education Policy Analysis Archives, 9,* 1–34.

Cochran-Smith, M., & Lytle, S. L. (1990). Research on teaching and teacher research: The issues that divide. *Educational Researcher, 19*(2), 2–11.

Cole, W. (2006, November 29). Some children left behind. *TIME.* Retrieved from http://www.time.com/time/nation/article/0,8599,1564101,00.html.

The College Board. (n.d.). *Students with disabilities.* Retrieved from http://professionals.collegeboard.com/testing/ssd.

Colvin, R. (2004). Public school choice: An overview. In F. M. Hess & C. E. Finn (Eds.), *Leaving no child behind: Options for kids in failing schools* (pp. 11–36). New York: Palgrave Macmillan.

Conrad, R. (1979). *The deaf school child: Language and cognitive function.* London: Harper and Row.

Corcoran, S., Evans, W. N., & Schwab, R. (2004). Women, the labor market, and the declining relative quality of teachers. *Journal of Policy Analysis and Management, 23,* 449–470.

Council for Exceptional Children. (2001). *What every special educator must know: The standards for the preparation and licensure of special educators* (4th ed.). Reston, VA: Author.

Council for Exceptional Children (2005). CEC knowledge and skills for beginning special education paraeducators: Knowledge and skills statements. Retrieved from http://www.cec.sped.org/Content/NavigationMenu/ProfessionalDevelopment/ProfessionalStandards/EthicsPracticeStandards/PS_paraks_check.pdf .

Council for Exceptional Children. (2005, March). *Resources on "highly qualified" requirements for special educators.* Reston, VA: Author.

Council for Exceptional Children. (2006). *New flexibility in testing students with disabilities: A positive step.* Retrieved from http://www.cec.sped.org/AM/Template.cfm?Section=Home&TEMPLATE=/CM/ContentDisplay.cfm&CONTENTID=6247.

Cross, C. (2004). *Political education: National policy comes of age.* New York: Teachers College Press.

Cuban, L. (2004). *The blackboard and the bottom line: Why schools can't be businesses.* Cambridge, MA: Harvard University Press.

Cullen, J., & Reback, R. (2006). Tinkering toward accolades: School gaming under a performance accountability system. In T. Gronberg and D. Jansen (Eds.), *Advances in applied microeconomics: Vol. 14. Improving school accountability: Checkups or choice* (pp. 1–34). Amsterdam: Elsevier Science.

Cummins, J. (1984). *Bilingualism and special education: Issues in assessment and pedagogy.* San Diego, CA: College-Hill.

Darling-Hammond, L. (2000). Teacher quality and student achievement: A review of state policy and evidence. *Education Policy Analysis Archives, 8.* Retrieved from http://epaa.asu.edu/ojs/article/viewFile/392/515.

Darling-Hammond, L., & Cobb, V. (1996). The changing context of teacher education. In F. B. Murray (Ed.), *The teacher educator's handbook: Building a knowledge base for the preparation of teachers* (pp. 14–59). San Francisco, CA: Jossey-Bass.

Darling-Hammond, L., & Sykes, G. (2003). Wanted: A national teacher supply policy for education: The right way to meet the "highly qualified teacher" challenge? *Education Policy Analysis Archives, 11.* Retrieved from http://epaa.asu.edu/ojs/article/viewFile/261/387.

Darling-Hammond, L., & Youngs, P. (2002). Defining "highly qualified teachers": What does "scientifically-based research" actually tell us? *Educational Researcher, 31*(9), 13–25.

DC School Choice Incentive Act of 2003 (Title III of Division C of the Consolidated Appropriations Act, 2004), Pub. L. 108-199 Stat. 3 (2004).

Dean, C., Lauer, P., & Urquhart, V. (2005). Outstanding teacher education programs: What do they have that the others don't? *Phi Delta Kappan, 87,* 284–289. Retrieved from http://www.kappanmagazine.org/content/87/4/284.abstract?ijkey=6589786ab851403cbdc82ee4261c3386bf8cfc01&keytype2=tf_ipsecsha.

De Stefano, L., & Metzer, D. (1991). High stakes testing and students with handicaps: An analysis of issues and policies. In R. E. Stake (Ed.), *Advances in program evaluation* (Vol. 1, pp. 267–288). Greenwich, CT: JAI Press.

Ding C., & Sherman, H. (2006). Teaching effectiveness and student achievement: Examining the relationship. *Educational Research Quarterly, 29*(4), 39–49.

Dolman, D. (2008). College and university requirements for teachers of the deaf at the undergraduate level: A twenty-year comparison. *American Annals of the Deaf, 153,* 322–327.

Duchesne, L., Sutton, A., & Bergeron, F. (2009). Language achievement in children who received cochlear implants between 1 and 2 years of age: Group trends and individual patterns. *Journal of Deaf Studies and Deaf Education, 14,* 465–485.

Easterbrooks, S. (1999). Improving practices for students with hearing impairments. *Exceptional Children, 65,* 537–554.

Easterbrooks, S. (2001). Veteran teachers of children who are deaf/hard of hearing describe language instructional practices: Implications for teacher preparation. *Teacher Education and Special Education, 24,* 116–127.

Eccarius, M. (1997). *Educating children who are deaf or hard of hearing: Assessment.* (ERIC Clearinghouse on Disabilities and Gifted Education Digest No. E550)

Education Commission of the States (ECS). (2004). *ECS Report to the nation: State implementation of the No Child Left Behind Act.* Denver, CO: Author. Retrieved from http://www.ecs.org/ecsmain.asp?page=/html/special/nclb/reporttothe nation/reporttothenation.htm.

Edwards, V. B. (Ed.). (2004, January 8). Quality counts 2004: Count me in—Special education in an era of standards. *Education Week, 23*(17). Retrieved from http://www.edweek.org/media/ew/qc/archives/QC04full.pdf.

Elementary and Secondary Education Act (ESEA) of 1965, Pub. L. 89-750, 20 U.S.C. 2701 *et seq.*

Elliott, S. N., & Braden, J. (2000). *Educational assessment and accountability for all students: Facilitating the meaningful participation of students with disabilities in district and statewide assessment programs.* Madison, WI: Wisconsin State Department of Public Instruction.

Elliott, S. N., Kratochwill, T. R., & McKevitt, B. (2001). Experimental analysis of the effects of testing accommodations on the scores of students with and without disabilities. *Journal of School Psychology, 39,* 3–24.

Elliott, S. N., McKevitt, B., & Kettler, R. (2002). Testing accommodations research and decision-making: The case of "good" scores being highly valued but difficult to achieve for all students. *Measurement and Evaluation in Counseling and Development, 35,* 153–166.

Erpenbach, W., Forte-Fast, E., & Potts, A. (2003, July). *Statewide educational accountability under NCLB.* Washington DC: Council of Chief State School Officers.

Evans, C. J. (2004). Educating deaf children in two languages. In D. Powers & G. Leigh (Eds.), *Educating deaf children: Global perspectives* (pp. 139–149). Washington, DC: Gallaudet University Press.

Ewoldt, C. (1990). The early literacy development of deaf children. In D. Moores & K. Meadow-Orlans (Eds.), *Educational and developmental aspects of deafness* (85–114). Washington, DC: Gallaudet University Press.

Family Educational Rights and Privacy Act (FERPA), 20 U.S.C. § 1232g; 34 CFR Part 99.

Feistritzer, C. E. (2005a). *Alternative routes to teacher certification: An overview.*

National Center for Education Information. Retrieved from http://www.ncei.com/Alt-Teacher-Cert.htm.

Feistritzer, C. E. (2005b). *A state-by-state analysis: 2005.* Washington, DC: National Center for Education Information.

Feller, B. (2006, August 17). Review: Teacher-quality mandate a big hurdle for states. *The Boston Globe.* Retrieved from http://www.boston.com/news/nation/articles/2006/08/17/review_teacher_quality_mandate_a_big_hurdle_for_states/, p. 2.

Florida Department of Education. (n.d.). *McKay Scholarship Program.* Tallahassee, FL: Author. Retrieved from http://www.floridaschoolchoice.org/Information/McKay/.

Flowers, C., Browder, D., Wakeman, S., & Karvonen, M. (2006*). Alternate assessment alignment pilot study: Report to the State Department of Education.* Charlotte, NC: University of North Carolina at Charlotte, National Alternate Assessment Center.

Foster, S., & Cue, K. (2009). Roles and responsibilities of itinerant specialist teachers of deaf and hard of hearing students. *American Annals of the Deaf, 153,* 435–449.

Freedman, S. (2006, October 11). Despite a doctorate and top students, unqualified to teach. *The New York Times.* Retrieved from http://www.nytimes.com/2006/10/11/education/11education.html.

Fuchs, L. S., & Fuchs, D. (1999). Fair and unfair testing accommodations. *School Administrator, 56*(10), 24–30.

Fulton, K., Yoon, I., & Lee, C. (2005, August). *Induction into learning communities.* Washington, DC: National Commission on Teaching and America's Future.

Gaetano, C. (2006, June 29). General education teachers face special education realities. *North Brunswick-South Brunswick* [New Jersey] *Sentinel.* Retrieved from http://www.nbs.gmnews.com/news/2006-06-29/Schools.

Gallagher, J. (1979). Minimum competency: The setting of educational standards. *Educational Evaluation and Policy Analysis, 1,* 62–67.

Gallaudet Research Institute. (2001). *Regional and national summary report of data from the 1999–2000 Annual Survey of Deaf and Hard of Hearing Children and Youth.* Washington, DC: Author.

Gallaudet Research Institute. (2005, January). *Regional and national summary report of data from the 2003–2004 Annual Survey of Deaf and Hard of Hearing Children and Youth.* Washington, DC: Author.

Gallaudet Research Institute. (2008). *Regional and national summary report of data from the 2007–08 annual survey of deaf and hard of hearing children and youth.* Washington, DC: Author.

Geers, A. (2002). Factors affecting the development of speech, language, and literacy in children with early cochlear implantation. *Language, Speech, and Hearing Services in Schools, 33,* 172–183.

Geers, A. E., & Brenner, C. A. (2004). Educational intervention and outcomes of early cochlear implantation. *International Congress Series, 1273,* 405–408.

Gerner de García, B. A. (1995). ESL applications for Hispanic deaf students. *Bilingual Research Journal, 19,* 452–467.

Gerner de Garcia, B. (2004). *Literacy for Latino deaf and hard of hearing English language learners: Building the knowledge base.* Presentation at the Gallaudet Research Institute Wednesday Seminar Series. Retrieved from http://research.gallaudet.edu/Presentations/2004-04-07-2.pdf.

Goldin-Meadow, S., & Mayberry, R. (2001). How do profoundly deaf children learn to read? *Learning Disabilities Research and Practice, 16,* 221–228.

Gordon, R., & Stump, K. (1996). Assessment of individuals with hearing impairments: Equity in testing procedures and accommodations. *Measurement and Evaluation in Counseling and Development, 29,* 111–119.

Graham, K. (2007, January 17). Andrews: Change No Child Left Behind Act. *Philadelphia Enquirer,* p. 1.

Granger, D. A. (2008). No Child Left Behind and the spectacle of failing schools: The mythology of contemporary school reform. *Educational Studies, 43,* 206–228.

Gratz, D. (2000). High standards for whom? *Phi Delta Kappan, 81,* 681–687.

Greenwood, C. R. (1991). A longitudinal analysis of time, engagement, and academic achievement in at-risk vs. non-risk students. *Exceptional Children, 57,* 521–535.

Greenwood, C. R., & Maheady, L. (1997). Measurable change in student performance: Forgotten standard in teacher preparation? *Teacher Education and Special Education, 20,* 265–275.

Guardino, C. (2008). Identification and placement for deaf students with multiple disabilities: Choosing the path less followed. *American Annals of the Deaf, 153,* 55–64.

Guiton, G., & Oakes, J. (1995). Opportunity to learn and conceptions of educational equality. *Educational Evaluation and Policy Analysis, 17,* 323–336.

Haertel, E. (1999). Performance assessment and education reform. *Phi Delta Kappan, 80,* 662–666.

Hannaway, J. (2004). Florida's implementation of the NCLB choice provisions: Confusions, constraints, and cascading scenarios. In F. M. Hess & C. E. Finn (Eds.), *Leaving no child behind: Options for kids in failing schools.* New York: Palgrave Macmillan.

Hanushek, E. (2001a). Deconstructing RAND. *Education Next, 1.* Retrieved from http://educationnext.org/randversusrand/.

Hanushek, E. (2001b). RAND versus RAND. *Education Next, 1.* Retrieved from http://educationnext.org/deconstructing-rand/.

Hanushek, E., & Raymond, M. (2003). Lessons about the design of state accountability systems. In P. Peterson & M. West (Eds.), *No Child Left Behind? The politics and practice of school accountability* (pp. 127–151). Washington, DC: Brookings Institution.

Hanushek, E., & Rivkin, S. G. (2004). How to improve the supply of high quality teachers. In D. Ravitch (Ed.), *Brookings papers on education policy 2004* (pp. 7–25). Washington, DC: Brookings Institution Press.

Hardman, M. L., & Dawson, S. (2008). The impact of federal public policy on curriculum and instruction for students with disabilities in the classroom. *Preventing School Failure, 52*(2), 5–11.

Harris, J., & Bamford, C. (2001). The uphill struggle: Services for deaf and hard of hearing people; Issues of equality, participation and access. *Disability & Society 16,* 969–980.

Hauser, P., O'Hearn, A., McKee, M., Steider, A., & Thew, D. (2010). Deaf epistemology: Deafhood and deafness. *American Annals of the Deaf, 154,* 486–492.

Henig, S. (2006, October 6). Back to school, for teachers: The No Child Left Behind Act has changed how colleges served classroom practitioners. *The Chronicle of Higher Education*, pp. A20–A22.

Herman, J. L., & Golan, S. (1993). The effects of standardized testing on teaching and schools. *Educational Measurement: Issues and Practice 12*(4), 20–25.

Herman, J. L., Klein, D. C., & Abedi, J. (2000). Assessing students' opportunity to learn: Teacher and student perspectives. *Educational Measurement: Issues and Practice, 19*(4), 16–24.

Hess, F. M. (2003). Refining or retreating? High-stakes accountability in the states. In P. Peterson, & M. West (Eds.), *No Child Left Behind? The politics and practice of school accountability* (pp. 55–79). Washington, DC: Brookings Institution.

Hess, F. M. (2006). Accountability without angst? Public opinion and No Child Left Behind. *Harvard Educational Review, 76,* 587–610.

Hess, F. M., & Brigham, F. (2000). None of the above: The promise and peril of high-stakes testing. *American School Board Journal, 187*(1), 26–29.

Hess, F. M., & Finn, C. E. (2004). *Leaving No Child Behind: Options for kids in failing schools.* New York: Palgrave Macmillan.

Hess, F. M., & Petrilli, M. (2006). *No Child Left Behind.* New York: Peter Lang Primer.

Heubert, J. P., & Hauser, R. M. (Eds.). (1999). *High stakes: Testing for tracking, promotion, and graduation.* Washington, DC: National Academy Press.

Hinde, E. (2003). The tyranny of the test: Elementary teachers' conceptualizations of the effects of state standards and mandated tests on their practice. *Current Issues in Education, 6*(10). Retrieved from http://cie.asu.edu/volume6/number10/index.html.

Hochschild, J. (2003). Rethinking accountability rules. In P. Peterson & M. West (Eds.), *No Child Left Behind? The politics and practice of school accountability* (pp. 107–126). Washington, DC: Brookings Institution Press.

Holcomb, T. K. (2010). Deaf epistemology: The deaf way of knowing. *American Annals of the Deaf, 154*, 471–478.

Holden-Pitt, L., & Diaz, J. (1998). Thirty years of annual survey of deaf and hard-of-hearing children and youth: A glance over the decades. *American Annals of the Deaf, 143*, 72–76.

Holt, J., Traxler, C., & Allen, T. (1992). *Interpreting the scores: A user's guide to the 8th edition Stanford Achievement Test for educators of deaf and hard-of-hearing students*. Washington, DC: Gallaudet University.

Honawar, V. (2006, May 16). Alternative routes for special education relieving shortages worsened by NCLB. *Education Week, 25*, 34.

Howell, J., & Luckner, J. (2003). Helping one deaf student develop content literacy skills: An action research report. *Communication Disorders Quarterly, 25*(1), 23–27.

Howell, W. (2004). Fumbling for an exit key: Parents, choice, and the future of NCLB. In F. M. Hess & C. E. Finn (Eds.), *Leaving No Child Behind: Options for kids in failing schools* (pp. 161–190). New York: Palgrave Macmillan.

Hughes, C., Guth, C., Hall, S., Presley, J., Dye, M., & Byers, C. (1999). They are my best friends: Peer buddies promote inclusion in high school. *Teaching Exceptional Children, 30*(4), 60–65.

Improving America's Schools Act (IASA) of 1994, Pub. L. 103-382, 108 Stat. 3518.

Individuals With Disabilities Education Act Amendments of 1997, 20 U.S.C. § 1400 *et seq.*

Individuals With Disabilities Education Act of 1990 (IDEA), Pub. L. 101-476, U.S.C.20 §§ 1400–1485.

Individuals With Disabilities Education Improvement Act (IDEIA) of 2004, Public Law 108-446, 118 Stat. 2647.

Ingersoll, R. (1998). The problem of out-of-field teaching. *Phi Delta Kappan, 79*, 773–776.

Ingersoll, R, (2001, January). A different approach to solving the teacher shortage problem (Teaching Quality Policy Briefs No. 3). Retrieved from the Center for the Study of Teaching and Policy Web site, http://depts.washington.edu/ctp mail/PDFs/Brief_three.pdf.

Ingersoll, R. (2005). The problem of underqualified teachers: A sociological perspective. *Sociology of Education, 78*, 175–178.

Jarvis, J. (2002). Exclusion by inclusion? Issues for deaf pupils and their mainstream teachers. *Education 3–13, 30*(2), 47–51.

Johnson, C., Benson, P., & Seaton, J. (1997). *Educational audiology handbook*. San Diego, CA: Singular Publishing Group.

Johnson, H. A. (2003a, February 6). *Teacher preparation within sensory impairments: Supply and demand, professional preparation and certification/licensure.*

Presentation given to Center on Personnel Studies in Special Education Research Design Panel, Washington, DC.

Johnson, H. A. (2003b). *U.S. deaf education teacher preparation programs: A look at the present and a vision for the future.* Gainesville, FL: Center on Personnel Studies in Special Education. Retrieved from http://www.docstoc.com/docs/55719429/Teacher-Preparation-win-Sensory-Impairments-Supply-Demand.

Johnson, R. C. (2004). Educational reform meets deaf education at national conference. *Sign Language Studies, 4,* 99–117.

Johnson, R. C., Liddell, S., & Erting, C. (1989). *Unlocking the curriculum: Principles for achieving access in deaf education.* Gallaudet Research Institute Working Paper No. 89-3. Washington, DC: Gallaudet University.

Kame'enui, E. J., Fuchs, L., Francis, D. J., Good, R., O'Connor, R. E., Simmons, D. C., Tindal, G., & Torgesen, J. (2006). The adequacy of tools for assessing reading competence: A framework and review. *Educational Researcher, 35*(4), 3–11.

Kampfer, S., Horvath, L., Kleinert, H., & Kearns, J. (2001). Teachers' perceptions of one state's alternate assessment: Implications for practice and preparation. *Exceptional Children, 67,* 361–374.

Karchmer, T., Allen, M., & Brown, S. (1988). *Deaf students and their schools: The changing demographics.* Washington, DC: Gallaudet Research Institute.

Kassini, I. (2008). Professionalism and coordination: Allies or enemies? *American Annals of the Deaf, 153,* 308–331.

Ketter, J., & Pool, J. (2001). Exploring the impact of a high-stakes direct writing assessment in two high school classrooms. *Research in the Teaching of English, 35,* 344–393.

Kieffer, M. J., Lesaux, N. K., Rivera, M., & Francis, D. J. (2009). Accommodations for English Language Learners taking large-scale assessments: A meta-analysis on effectiveness and validity. *Review of Educational Research*, 29, 1168–1201.

King, L. (2007, January 18). Program to identify most dangerous schools misses mark. *USA Today,* p. 3. Retrieved from http://www.usatoday.com/news/education/2007-01-18-dangerousschools_x.htm.

Kingsbury, G. G., Olson, A., Cronin, J., Hauser, C., & Houser, R. (2004). *The state of state standards: Research investigating proficiency levels in fourteen states.* Report from the Northwest Evaluation Association. Lake Oswego, OR: Northwest Evaluation Association.

Kleinert, H. L., & Kearns, J. F. (1999). A validation study of the performance indicators and learner outcomes of Kentucky's alternate assessment for students with significant disabilities. *The Journal of the Association for Persons With Severe Handicaps, 24,* 100–110.

Kleinhenz, E., & Ingvarson, L. (2004). Teacher accountability in Australia: Current policies and practices and their relation to the improvement of teaching and learning. *Research Papers in Education, 19,* 31–49.

Kluwin, T., Morris, C., & Clifford, J. (2004). A rapid ethnography of itinerant teachers of the deaf. *American Annals of the Deaf, 149,* 62–72.

Koretz, D., & Barton, K. (2003). *Assessing students with disabilities: Issues and evidence.* Technical report for the Center for the Study of Evaluation, National Center for Research on Evaluation, Standards and Student Testing (CRESST). Los Angeles, CA: CRESST.

Kornhaber, M., & Orfield, G. (2001). *Raising standards or raising barriers: Inequality and high stakes testing in public education.* New York: Century Foundation Press.

Kuntze, M. (1998). Literacy and deaf children: The language question. *Topics in Language Disorders, 18*(4), 1–15.

Kupermintz, H. (2002). Teacher effects as a measure of teacher effectiveness: Construct validity considerations in TVAAS (Tennessee Value-Added Assessment System). Center of the Study of Evaluation Technical Report No. 563. Los Angeles, CA: University of California, National Center for Research on Evaluation.

Kushalnagar, P., Hannay, H. J., & Hernandez, A. (2010). Bilingualism and attention: A study of balanced and unbalanced bilingual deaf users of American Sign Language and English. *Journal of Deaf Studies and Deaf Education, 15,* 263–273.

Ladson-Billings, G. (2006). Presidential address: From the achievement gap to the education debt: Understanding achievement in U.S. schools. Webcast retrieved from http://www.cmcgc.com/Media/MWP/260407/49_10_files/ http://www .aera.net/Default.aspx?id=6112.

Lane, H. (1999). *The mask of benevolence: Disabling the deaf community* (2nd ed.). San Diego: DawnSignPress.

Lang, H. G. (2002). Higher education for deaf students: Research priorities in the new millennium. *Journal of Deaf Studies and Deaf Education, 7,* 267–280.

LaSasso, C., & Metzger, M. (1998). An alternate route for preparing deaf children for BiBi programs: The home language as L1 and cued speech for conveying traditionally-spoken languages. *Journal of Deaf Studies and Deaf Education, 3,* 265–289.

LaSasso, C., & Wilson, A. (2000). Results of two national surveys of leadership personnel needs in deaf education. *American Annals of the Deaf, 145,* 429–435.

Laurence, H. (1991). The bilingual/bicultural education of deaf individuals: A Vygotskian perspective. *Teaching English to Deaf and Second-Language Students, 9,* 10–13.

Laurent Clerc National Deaf Education Center. (2001). *What is the Standards for Achievement Project?* Washington, DC: Gallaudet University.

Lazarus, S. S., Thurlow, M. L., Lail, K. E., Eisenbraun, K. D., & Kato, K. (2006). *2005 state policies on assessment participation and accommodations for students with disabilities* (Synthesis Report No. 64). Minneapolis, MN: University of Minnesota, National Center on Educational Outcomes. Retrieved from http://education .umn.edu/NCEO/OnlinePubs/Synthesis64/.

Lee, J. (2004). How feasible is adequate yearly progress (AYP)? Simulations of school AYP "uniform averaging" and "safe harbor" under the No Child Left Behind Act. *Education Policy Analysis Archives, 12.* Retrieved http://epaa.asu.edu/ojs/article/view/169.

Lee-Tarver, A. (2006). Are individualized education plans a good thing? A survey of teachers' perceptions of the utility of IEPs in regular education settings. *Journal of Instructional Psychology, 33,* 263–272.

Levine, A. (2006). *Educating school teachers.* Washington, DC: Education School Project.

Linn, R. L. (2003a). Accountability: Responsibility and reasonable expectations. *Educational Researcher, 32*(7), 3–13.

Linn, R. L. (2003b). Performance standards: Utility for different uses of assessments. *Education Policy Analysis Archives, 11.* Retrieved from http://epaa.asu.edu/ojs/article/view/259/385.

Linn, R. L. (2005a). Conflicting demands of No Child Left Behind and state systems: Mixed messages about school performance. *Education Policy Analysis Archives, 13.* Retrieved from http://epaa.asu.edu/ojs/article/view/138/264.

Linn, R. L. (2005b). *Fixing the NCLB accountability system* (CRESST Policy Brief No. 8). Los Angeles: University of California, National Center for Research on Evaluation, Standards, and Student Testing.

Loeterman, M., Paul, P. V., & Donahue, S. (2002, February). Reading and deaf children. *Reading Online, 5*(6). Retrieved from http://www.readingonline.org/articles/art_index.asp?HREF=loeterman/index.html.

Lollis, J., & LaSasso, C. (2009). The appropriateness of the NC state-mandated reading competency test for deaf students as a criterion for high school graduation. *Journal of Deaf Studies and Deaf Education, 14,* 76–98.

Luckner, J. (1991). Skills needed for teaching hearing-impaired adolescents. *American Annals of the Deaf, 136,* 422–427.

Luckner, J. (1992). Preparing teachers to work with adolescent students who are hearing impaired: A survey of training programs. *Teacher Education and Special Education, 15,* 25–31.

Luckner, J., & Bowen, S. (2006). Assessment practices of professionals serving students who are deaf or hard of hearing: An initial investigation. *American Annals of the Deaf, 151,* 410–417.

Luckner, J., & Cooke, C. (2010). A summary of the vocabulary research with students who are deaf or hard of hearing. *American Annals of the Deaf, 155,* 38–67.

Luckner, J., & Handley, C. (2008). A summary of the reading comprehension research undertaken with students who are deaf or hard of hearing. *American Annals of the Deaf, 153,* 6–36.

Luckner, J. L., & Muir, S. (2002). Suggestions for helping students who are deaf succeed in general education settings. *Communication Disorders Quarterly, 24*(1), 22–30.

Lytle, R., & Rovins, M. (1997). Reforming deaf education: A paradigm shift from how to teach to what to teach. *American Annals of the Deaf, 142,* 7–15.

Maranto, R., & Maranto, A. (2004). Options for low-income students: Evidence from the states. In F. M. Hess & C. E. Finn (Eds.), *Leaving no child behind: Options for kids in failing schools* (pp. 63–88). New York: Palgrave Macmillan.

Marschark, M., & Humphries, T. (2010). Deaf studies by any other name? *Journal of Deaf Studies and Deaf Education, 15,* 1–2.

Marschark, M., Lang, H., & Albertini, J. (2002). *Educating deaf students: From research to practice.* New York: Oxford University Press.

Marschark, M., Sapere, P., Covertino, C., Mayer, C., Wauters, L., & Sarchet, T. (2009). Are deaf students' reading challenges really about reading? *American Annals of the Deaf, 154,* 357–370.

Marschark, M., & Spencer, P. E. (2006). Spoken language development of deaf and hard-of-hearing children: Historical and theoretical perspectives. In P. E. Spencer & M. Marschark (Eds.), *Advances in the spoken language development of deaf and hard-of-hearing children* (pp. 3–21). New York: Oxford University Press.

Martin, D., & Lytle, R. (2000). Deaf teacher candidates in hearing classrooms: A unique teacher preparation program. *American Annals of the Deaf, 145,* 15–21.

Maxwell, M. (1986). Beginning reading and deaf children. *American Annals of the Deaf, 131,* 14–20.

Mayer, C., & Akamatsu, C. T. (1999). Bilingual-bicultural models of literacy education for deaf students: Considering the claims. *Journal of Deaf Studies and Deaf Education, 4,* 1–8.

McCartney, B. D. (1994). Inclusion as a practical matter. *American Annals of the Deaf, 139,* 161–162.

McCleskey, J., Tyler, N., & Flippin, S. (2004). The supply and demand for special education teachers: A review of research regarding the chronic shortage of special education teachers. *Journal of Special Education, 38,* 5–21.

McCombs, J., Kirby, S., Barney, H., Darilek, H., & Magee, S. (2004). *Achieving state and national literacy goals: A long uphill road.* Santa Monica, CA: RAND.

McDermid, C. (2009). Social construction of American Sign Language—English interpreters. *Journal of Deaf Studies and Deaf Education, 14,* 105–130.

McDermott, K. A. (2003). What causes variation in states' accountability policies? *Peabody Journal of Education, 78*(4), 153–176.

McDonnell, L., McLaughlin, M., & Morison, P. (1997). *Educating one and all: Students with disabilities and standards-based reform.* Washington, DC: National Academy Press.

McDonnell, L. M. (2005). No Child Left Behind and the federal role in education: Evolution or revolution? *Peabody Journal of Education, 80*(4), 19–38.

McGrew, K., Thurlow, M., Shriner, J., & Spiegel, A. (1992*). Inclusion of students with disabilities in national and state data collection programs* (Technical Report No. 2). Minneapolis, MN: National Center on Educational Outcomes.

McKevitt, B., & Elliott, S. N. (2003). Effects and perceived consequences of using read aloud and teacher-recommended testing accommodations on a reading achievement test. *The School Psychology Review, 32,* 583–600.

Medler, A. (2004). Colorado: Layered reforms and challenges of scale. In F. M. Hess & C. E. Finn (Eds.), *Leaving no child behind: Options for kids in failing schools* (113–136). New York: Palgrave Macmillan.

Messick, S. (1995). Validity of psychological assessment: Validation of inferences from persons' responses and performances as scientific inquiry into score meaning. *American Psychologist, 50,* 741–749.

Miller, M., Strosnider, R., & Dooley, E. (2002). States' diversity requirements for teachers. *Teacher Education and Special Education, 25,* 32–40.

Minnema, J., Thurlow, M., Anderson, M., & Stone, K. (2005). *English language learners with disabilities and large-scale assessments: What the literature can tell us.* (ELLs with Disabilities Report No. 6). Minneapolis, MN: University of Minnesota, National Center on Educational Outcomes. Retrieved from http://education.umn.edu/NCEO/OnlinePubs/ELLsDisReport6.html.

Minnesota State Department of Education. (2010). *2010 Minnesota academic standards in English language arts K–12.* Roseville, MN: Author. Retrieved from http://education.state.mn.us/MDE/Academic_Excellence/Academic_Standards/index.html.

Mitchell, R. (2004). National profile of deaf and hard of hearing students in special education from weighted survey results. *American Annals of the Deaf, 149,* 336–349.

Mitchell, R. (2005). *Can you tell me how many deaf persons there are in the United States?* Retrieved from http://research.gallaudet.edu/Demographics/factsheet.php#Q1.

Mitchell, R., & Karchmer, M. (2004). Chasing the mythical ten percent: Parental hearing status of deaf and hard of hearing children in the United States. *Sign Language Studies, 4,* 138–163.

Mitchell, R., & Karchmer, M. (2005, April). *Finding and collecting data from a shrinking and dispersed population.* Presentation as part of the symposium Pebbles in the Mainstream: The Future of Research in the Education of the Deaf, annual meeting of the American Educational Research Association, Montreal.

Mitchell, R., & Karchmer, M. (2006). Demographics of deaf education: More students in more places. *American Annals of the Deaf, 151,* 95–104.

Moe, T. (2003). Politics, control, and the future of school accountability. In P. Peterson & M. West (Eds.), *No Child Left Behind? The politics and practice of school accountability* (pp. 80–106). Washington, DC: Brookings Institution.

Moog, J. (2002). Changing expectations for children with cochlear implants. *Annals of Otology, Rhinology and Laryngology, 111,* 138–142.

Moon, T. R., Callahan, C. M., & Tomlinson, C. A. (2003, April 28). Effects of state testing programs on elementary schools with high concentrations of student poverty—good news or bad news? *Current Issues in Education, 6*(8). Retrieved from http://cie.ed.asu.edu/volume6/number8/.

Moores, D. (1991). The great debates: Where, how, and what to teach deaf children. *American Annals of the Deaf, 136,* 35–37.

Moores, D. (2004). The future of education of deaf children: The implications of population projects. *American Annals of the Deaf, 149,* 3–4.

Moores, D. (2006). Comments on "W(h)ither the Deaf community." *Sign Language Studies, 6,* 202–209.

Moores, D. (Ed.). (2008a). Reference issue. *American Annals of the Deaf, 153.*

Moores, D. (2008b). Research on bi-bi instruction. *American Annals of the Deaf, 153,* 3–4.

Moores, D. (2009). Cochlear failures. *American Annals of the Deaf, 153,* 423–424.

Moores, D. F., & Miller, M. S. (2001). Literacy publications: *American Annals of the Deaf* 1996 to 2000. *American Annals of the Deaf, 146,* 77–80.

Muller, E. (2005a). *Alternative routes to certification for special educators.* Alexandria, VA: National Association of State Directors of Special Education, Project Forum.

Muller, E. (2005b). *Deaf and hard of hearing: State infrastructures and programs.* Alexandria, VA: National Association of State Directors of Special Education, Project Forum.

Musselman, C. (2000). How do children who can't hear learn to read and alphabetic script? A review of the literature on reading and deafness. *Journal of Deaf Studies and Deaf Education, 5,* 9–31.

Mutua, N. K., & Elhoweris, H. (2002). Parents' expectations about the post-school outcomes of children with hearing impairments. *Exceptionality, 10,* 189–201.

Myers, S., & Fernandes, J. (2009). Deaf studies: A critique of the predominant U.S. theoretical direction. *Journal of Deaf Studies and Deaf Education, 15,* 30–49. doi: 10.1093/deafed/enp017.

National Assessment of Educational Progress. (2000). *Reading framework for the National Assessment of Educational Progress: 1992–2000.* Washington, DC: National Assessment Governing Board.

National Center on Education Outcomes. (1998). *Accountability for the results of educating students with disabilities: Assessment conference report on the new assessment provisions of the 1997 amendments to the Individuals with Disabilities Education Act.* Minneapolis, MN: Author.

National Center on Education Statistics. (2006). *The condition of education 2006* (NCES No. 2006–071). Washington, DC: Author.

National Center on Low-Incidence Disabilities. (2006). *Student proficiency scores.* Retrieved from www.nclid.unco.edu.

National Center on Low-Incidence Disabilities (Now the National Center on Severe and Sensory Disabilities). (2007). *State assessment results for students with low incidence disabilities.* Greeley, CO: Author. Retrieved from http://www.unco.edu/ncssd/ResearchSummit/Resources/outcomes.pdf .

National Commission on Excellence in Education. (1983). *A nation at risk: The imperative for educational reform.* Washington, DC: Author.

National Education Association. (2006). *School vouchers position statement.* Washington, DC: Author.

National Reading Panel. (2000). *Teaching children to read: An evidence-based assessment of the scientific research literature on reading and its implications for reading instruction.* Washington, DC: Author.

Neal, D., & Schanzenbach, K., (2007). *Left behind by design: Proficiency counts and test-based accountability* (NBER Working Paper Series No. 13293). Cambridge, MA: National Bureau of Economic Research.

Newmann, F. M., & Wehlage, G. G. (1995). Successful school restructuring: A report to the public and educators. Washington DC: American Federation of Teachers. (ERIC Document Reproduction Service No ED387925)

New Mexico State Department of Education. (2008*). Consolidated state application accountability workbook.* Washington, DC: U.S. Department of Education. Retrieved from: http://www2.ed.gov/admins/lead/account/stateplans03/index .html.

Nielsen, D. C., & Luetke-Stahlman, B. (2002). Phonological awareness: One key to the reading proficiency of deaf children. *American Annals of the Deaf, 147,* 11–19.

Niparko, J., & Blankenhorn, R. (2003). Cochlear implants in young children. *Mental Retardation and Developmental Disabilities Research Reviews, 9,* 267–275.

No Child Left Behind Act of 2001, 20 U.S.C. 6301 *et seq.*

North Carolina State Board of Education. (n.d.). *Policy manual.* Retrieved from http://www.ncpublicschools.org/schoolsafety/resources/violence/dangerous/.

North Central Regional Educational Laboratory. (2002). *The impact of alternative certification in the midwest.* Retrieved from http://www.ncrel.org/policy/pubs/ html/pivol12/nov2002d.htm.

Novak, J. R., & Fuller, B. (2003, December). *Penalizing diverse schools?* Policy Brief for Policy Analysis for California Education (PACE). Retrieved from http:// pace.berkeley.edu/2003/12/01/penalizing-diverse-schools-similar-test-scores -but-different-students-bring-federal-sanctions/.

Nussbaum, D., LaPorta, R., & Hinger, J. (2003). (Eds.). *Cochlear implants and sign language: Putting it all together.* Washington, DC: Gallaudet University.

Odden, A. R., Borman, G., & Fermanich, M. (2004). Assessing teacher, classroom, and school effects, including fiscal effects. *Peabody Journal of Education, 79*(4), 4–32.

Olson, L. (2002, April 18). 'Inadequate' yearly gains are predicted. *Education Week.* Retrieved from http://www.edweek.org/ew/articles/2002//04/03/29ayp.h21 .html.

Olson, L. (2005a, September 21). AYP rules miss many in special education. *Education Week, 25,* 1, 24.

Olson, L. (2005b, September 7). Defying predictions, state trends prove mixed on schools making NCLB targets. *Education Week, 25*(2).

Pagliaro, C. (1998). Mathematics preparation and professional development of deaf education teachers. *American Annals of the Deaf, 143,* 373–379.

Palmer, S., & Coleman, A. (2004, February). *Blueprint for building a single statewide accountability system.* Washington, DC: Council of Chief State School Officers.

Paul. P. V. (1994). Response to unlocking the curriculum: Principles for achieving access in deaf education. *Teaching English to Deaf and Second-Language Students, 10,* 18–21.

Paul, P. V. (1997). Reading for students with hearing impairments: Research review and implications. *Volta Review, 99,* 73–87.

Paul, P., & Moores, D. (2010). Perspectives on *Deaf* epistemologies. *American Annals of the Deaf 154,* 417–420.

Paul, P. V., Wang, Y., Trezek, B., & Luckner, J. (2009). Phonology is necessary, but not sufficient: A rejoinder. *American Annals of the Deaf, 154,* 346–356.

Peske, H., & Haycock, K. (2006, June). *Teaching inequality: How poor and minority students are shortchanged on teacher quality.* Washington, DC: Education Trust.

Phillips, S. E. (1994). High-stakes testing accommodations: Validity versus disabled rights. *Applied Measurement in Education, 7*(2), 93–120.

Pitoniak, M. J., & Royer, J. M. (2001). Testing accommodations for examinees with disabilities: A review of psychometric, legal, and social policy issues. *Review of Educational Research, 71*(1), 53–104.

Plank, D. N., Dunbar, C., Jr. (2004). *False start in Michigan:* The early implementation of the federal "No Child Left Behind" Act. In F. Hess & C. Finn (Eds.), *Leaving no child left behind: Options for kids in failing schools.* New York: Palgrave Macmillan.

Popham, W. J. (2004). *America's "failing" schools. How parents and teachers can cope with No Child Left Behind.* NY: Routledge.

Porter, A. C. (1989). External standards and good teaching: The pros and cons of telling teachers what to do. *Educational Evaluation and Policy Analysis, 11,* 343–356.

Porter, A. C. (2002). Measuring the content of instruction: Uses in research and practice. *Educational Researcher, 31*(7), 3–14.

Porter-Magee, K. (2004, September/October). Teacher quality, controversy, and NCLB. *The Clearing House, 78*(1), 26–29. Heldref Publications.

Power, D., Hyde, M., & Leigh, G. (2008). Learning English from signed English: An impossible task? *American Annals of the Deaf, 153,* 37–47.

Powers, A., & Elliott, R. (1990). Preparation of teachers who serve hearing impaired students with additional mild handicaps. *Teacher Education and Special Education, 13,* 200–202.

Powers, S. (2001). Investigating good practice in supporting deaf pupils in mainstream schools. *Educational Review, 53,* 181–189.

Qi, S., & Mitchell, R. E. (2007, April 10). *Large-scale academic achievement testing of deaf and hard-of-hearing students: Past, present, and future.* Paper presented at the annual meeting of the American Educational Research Association, Chicago, Illinois.

Qualls-Mitchell, P. (2002). Reading enhancement for deaf and hard of hearing children through multicultural empowerment. *The Reading Teacher, 56*(1), 76–84.

Quenemoen, R., Rigney, S., & Thurlow, M. (2002). Use of alternate assessment results in reporting and accountability systems: Conditions for use based on research and practice (Synthesis Report No. 43). Minneapolis, MN: University of Minnesota, National Center on Educational Outcomes. Retrieved from http://education.umn.edu/NCEO/OnlinePubs/Synthesis43.html.

Quenemoen, R., & Thurlow, M., (2002). *Including alternate assessment results in accountability decisions* (Policy Directions No. 13). Minneapolis, MN: University of Minnesota, National Center on Educational Outcomes. Retrieved from http://www.cehd.umn.edu/NCEO/OnlinePubs/archive/Policy/Policy13.htm.

Rabalate, P. (2006, August). *Statement to the Aspen Institute's Commission on No Child Left Behind.* Washington, DC: National Education Association.

Ramsey, C. (1997). *Deaf children in public schools: Placement, context and consequences.* Washington, DC: Gallaudet University Press.

Rebell, M., & Wolff, J. (2008). *Moving every child ahead: From NCLB hype to meaningful educational opportunity.* New York: Teachers College Press.

Registry of Interpreters for the Deaf. (2009). *Educational interpreter resources toolkit.* Written and compiled by the Educational Interpreting Committee 2007–2009. Alexandria, VA: Author. Retrieved from http://www.rid.org/UserFiles/File/pdfs/About_RID/For_Educational_Interpreters/Educational_Interpreting_Resources_Toolkit/Educational_Interpreting_ToolKit(1).pdf.

Rehabilitation Act of 1973, U.S.C. § 701 *et seq.*

Ronnberg, J. (2003). Cognition in the hearing impaired and deaf as a bridge between signal and dialogue: A framework and a model. *International Journal of Audiology, 42,* 68–76.

Rosenberg, M., & Sindelar, P. (2005). The proliferation of alternative routes to certification in special education: A critical review of the literature. *Journal of Special Education, 39,* 117–127.

Sable, J., & Hill, J. (2006). *Overview of public elementary and secondary students, staff, schools, school districts, revenues, and expenditures: School year 2004–05 and fiscal year 2004* (NCES 2007-309). Washington, DC: U.S. Department of Education, National Center for Education Statistics.

Sanchez, C. (July 6, 2006). *California schools could lose aid over 'No Child' law.* News report for *All Things Considered* on National Public Radio. Retrieved from http://www.npr.org/templates/story/story.php?storyId=5538536.

Saunders, J. (1997). Educating deaf and hearing children in a bilingual environment. *Canadien Academie for Education of the Deaf and Hard of Hearing (23),* 61–68.

Scheetz, N., & Martin, S. (2006). Teacher quality: A comparison of national board-certified and non-board-certified teachers of deaf students. *American Annals of the Deaf, 151,* 71–86.

Schemo, D. (2004, August, 30). School achievement reports often exclude the disabled. *New York Times.* http://query.nytimes.com/gst/fullpage.html?res=9D03 E7D71F3EF933A0575BC0A9629C8B63.

Schick, B., & Williams, K. (2001). The educational interpreter performance assessment: Evaluating interpreters who work with children. *Odyssey* (Winter/Spring), 12. Retrieved from http://ccdam.gallaudet.edu/pdf/ed-terp-performance.pdf.

Schimmel, C., Edwards, S., & Prickett, H. (1999). Reading? . . . Pah! (I got it!): Innovative reading techniques for successful deaf readers. *American Annals of the Deaf, 144,* 298–308.

Schirmer, B. (2000). *Language and literacy development in children who are deaf* (2nd ed.). Needham Heights, MA: Allyn and Bacon.

Schirmer, B. (2008). How effectively are we preparing teacher educators in special education? The case of deaf education. *American Annals of the Deaf, 153,* 411–419.

Schirmer, B., Bailey, J., & Lockman, A. (2004). What verbal protocols reveal about the reading strategies of deaf students: A replication study. *American Annals of the Deaf, 149,* 5–17.

Schirmer, B., & McGough, S. (2005). Teaching reading to children who are deaf: Do the conclusions of the National Reading Panel apply? *Review of Educational Research, 75*(1), 83–117.

Schrag, J. (2003). No Child Left Behind and its implications for students with disabilities. *The Special Edge, 16*(2), 1–4.

Scruggs, T., & Mastropieri, M. (1996). Teacher perceptions of mainstreaming/inclusion, 1958–1995: A research synthesis. *Exceptional Children, 63,* 59–75.

Shaw, S., & Roberson, L. (2009). Service-learning recentering the deaf community in interpreter education. *American Annals of the Deaf, 154,* 277–283.

Shepard. L. A. (1993). Evaluating test validity. *Review of Research in Education, 19,* 405–450.

Shriner, J., & DeStefano, L. (2003). Participation and accommodation in state assessment: The role of Individualized Education Programs. *Exceptional Children, 69,* 147–161.

Shroyer, E., & Compton, M. (1992). Reforming teacher education: A model program for preparing teachers of deaf children. *American Annals of the Deaf, 137,* 416–419.

Siegel, L. (2000). The educational and communication needs of deaf and hard of hearing children: A statement of principle on fundamental educational change. *American Annals of the Deaf, 145,* 64–77.

Siegel, L. (2002). The argument for a constitutional right to communication and language. *Journal of Deaf Studies and Deaf Education, 7,* 258–266. doi: 10.1093/deafed/7.3.258.

Siegel, L. (2005, April). *The legal right to communication in America*. Presentation at the Gallaudet Research Institute Wednesday Seminar Series. Retrieved from http://research.gallaudet.edu/Presentations.

Silverman, J. (2006, July 26). School closures for disabled causes worry. *The New Orleans Times-Picayune*.

Simms, L., & Thumann, H. (2007). In search of a new, linguistically and culturally sensitive paradigm in deaf education. *American Annals of the Deaf, 152,* 302–331.

Simpson, M. A., Gong, B., & Marion, S. (2006). *Effect of minimum cell sizes and confidence interval sizes for special education subgroups on school-level AYP determinations* (Synthesis Report No. 61). Minneapolis, MN: University of Minnesota, National Center on Educational Outcomes. Retrieved from http://education.umn.edu/NCEO/OnlinePubs/Synthesis61.html.

Smith, M. L., Miller-Kahn, L., Heinecke, W., & Jarvis, P. (2004). *Political spectacle and the rate of American schools.* New York: Routledge Falmer.

Soar, R. S., Medley, D. M., & Coker, H. (1983). Teacher evaluation: A critique of currently used methods. *Phi Delta Kappan, 65,* 239–246.

South East Regional Resource Center. (2004). *Regional personnel preparation model.* Montgomery, AL: Author.

Spaulding, S., Carolino, B., & Amen, K-A. (2004). *Immigrant students and secondary school reform: Compendium of best practices.* Washington, DC: Council of Chief State School Officers.

Speer, P., & Hughey, J. (1995). Community organizing: An ecological route to empowerment and power. *American Journal of Community Psychology, 23,* 729–748. doi: 10.1007/BF02506989.

Steffan, R. (2004). Navigating the difficult waters of the No Child Left Behind Act of 2001: What it means for education of the deaf. *American Annals of the Deaf, 149,* 46–50.

Stinson, M. S., & Antia, S. D. (1999). Considerations in educating deaf and hard-of-hearing students in inclusive settings. *Journal of Deaf Studies and Deaf Education, 4,* 163–175.

Storbeck, C., & Calvert-Evans, J. (2008). Towards integrated practices in early detection of and intervention for deaf and hard of hearing children. *American Annals of the Deaf, 153,* 314–332.

Stuckless, R. (1991). Reflections on bilingual, bicultural education for deaf children: Some concerns about current advocacy and trends. *American Annals of the Deaf, 136,* 270–272.

Stullich, S., Eisner, E., McCrary, J., & Roney, C. (2006). *National assessment of Title 1: Interim report to Congress.* Retrieved from http://www2ed.gov/rschstat/eval/disadv/title1interimreport/index.html.

Sullivan, P., & Schulte, L. (1992). Factor analysis of WISC-R with deaf and hard-of-hearing children. *Psychological Assessment, 4,* 537–540.

Temin, P. (2002). Teacher quality and the future of America. *Eastern Economic Journal, 28,* 285–300.

Thompson, S. J., Johnstone, C. J., Thurlow, M. L., & Altman, J. R. (2005). *2005 state special education outcomes: Steps forward in a decade of change.* Minneapolis, MN: University of Minnesota, National Center on Educational Outcomes.

Thompson, S. J., Johnstone, C. J., Thurlow, M. L., & Clapper, A. T. (2004). *State literacy standards, practice, and testing: Exploring accessibility* (Technical Report No. 38). Minneapolis, MN: University of Minnesota, National Center on Educational Outcomes. Retrieved from http://education.umn.edu/NCEO/OnlinePubs/Technical38.htm.

Thompson, S., & Thurlow, M. (2003). *2001 State special education outcomes: A report on state activities at the beginning of a new decade.* Minneapolis, MN: University of Minnesota, National Center on Educational Outcomes. Retrieved from http://education.umn.edu/NCEO/OnlinePubs/2001StateReport.html.

Thurlow, M. L., & Wiley, H. I. (2004). *Almost there in public reporting of assessment results for students with disabilities* (Technical Report No. 39). Minneapolis, MN: University of Minnesota, National Center on Educational Outcomes.

Tice, P., Chapman, C., Princiotta, D., & Bielick, S. (2006). Trends in the use of school choice: 1993–2003 (National Center for Education Statistics Report No. 2007045). Washington, DC: U.S. Department of Education, National Center for Education Statistics.

Tindal, G., & Fuchs, L. (2000). *A summary of research on test changes: An empirical basis for defining accommodations.* Lexington, KY: Mid-South Regional Resource Center.

Tomblin, J. B., Spencer, L., Flock, S., Tyler, R., & Gantz, B. (1999). A comparison of language achievement in children with cochlear implants and children using hearing aids. *Journal of Speech, Language, and Hearing Research, 42,* 497–509.

Toplikar, D. (2006, August 27). Special education teachers in chronically short supply. *Lawrence Journal-World,* p. 4. Retrieved from http://www2.ljworld.com/news/2006/aug/27/special_education_teachers_chronically_short_suppl/.

Toppo, G. (2007, January 8). How Bush education law has changed our schools. *USA Today,* p. 4. Retrieved from http://www.usatodaycom/news/education/2007-01-07-no-child_x.htm.

Tough, P. (2006, November 26). What it takes to make a student. *New York Times.* Retrieved from http://www.nytimes.com/2006/11/26/magazine/26tough.html?_r=1.

Towles, E. A., Garrett, B., Burdette, P., & Burdge, M. (2003). *What are the consequences of large-scale alternate assessment systems and their influence on instruction?* (ERIC Document Reproduction Service No. ED035081)

Traxler, C. (2000). The Stanford Achievement Test, 9th Edition: National norming and performance standards for deaf and hard-of-hearing students. *Journal of Deaf Studies and Deaf Education, 5,* 337–348.

Trezek, B., & Wang, Y, (2006). Implications of utilizing a phonics-based reading curriculum with children who are deaf or hard of hearing. *Journal of Deaf Studies and Deaf Education 11*, 202–213. Retrieved from http://jdsde.oxfordjournals.org/content/11/2/202.full.

Truax, R. R., Sue Fan, F., & Whitesell, K. (2004). Literacy learning: Meeting the needs of children who are deaf or hard of hearing with additional special needs. *Volta Review, 104*, 307–326.

Turner, M., Baldwin, L., Kleinert, H., & Kearns, J. (2000). An examination of the concurrent validity of Kentucky's alternate assessment system. *Journal of Special Education, 34*, 69–76.

U.S. Department of Education. (2003). *Consolidated state application accountability workbook*. Washington, DC: Author.

U.S. Department of Education. (2007a). *Secretary Spellings invites eligible states to submit innovative models for expanded growth model pilot*. Retrieved from http://www2.ed.gov/news/pressreleases/2007/12/12072007.htm.

U.S. Department of Education. (2007b). *Modified academic achievement standards: Non-regulatory guidance*. Washington, DC: Author. Retrieved from http://www.ed.gov/policy/speced/guid/nclb/twopercent.doc.

U.S. Department of Health and Human Services, Office of Civil Rights. (n.d.). *Your rights under Section 504 of the Rehabilitation Act*. Retrieved from http://www.hhs.gov/ocr/504.html.

U.S. Department of Justice, Division of Civil Rights. (2005, September). *A guide to disability rights laws*. Retrieved from www.usdoj.gov/crt/ada/cguide.pdf.

U.S. Food and Drug Administration. (2004). *Cochlear implants*. Washington, DC: Author. Retrieved from http://www.fda.gov/cdrh/cochlear/whatare.html.

U.S. General Accounting Office (GAO). (2001). *School vouchers publicly funded programs in Cleveland and Milwaukee* (GAO-01-914). Report to the Honorable Judd Gregg, U.S. Senate. Retrieved from http://www.gao.gov/new.items/d01914.pdf.

U.S. Office of Special Education Programs. (2004). *IDEA Part B child count table AA3. Number served (ages 6–21), by disability and state*. Washington, DC: Author.

U.S. Office of Special Education Programs. (2007). *29th annual report to Congress on the Individuals with Disabilities Education Act (IDEA), Part D*. Retrieved from http://www2.ed.gov/about/reports/annual/osep/2007/part-d/idea-part-d-2007.pdf.

Van Cleve, J. V., & Crouch, B. A. (1989). *A place of their own*. Washington, DC: Gallaudet University Press.

Van Getson, G., Minnema, J., & Thurlow, M. (2004). *Rapid changes, repeated challenges: States' out-of-level testing policies for 2003–2004* (Out-of-Level Testing

Project Report No. 13). Minneapolis, MN: University of Minnesota, National Center on Educational Outcomes. Retrieved from http://education.umn.edu/NCEO/OnlinePubs/OOLT13.html.

Vernon, M., & Rhodes, A. (2009). Deafness and autistic spectrum disorders. *American Annals of the Deaf, 154,* 5–14.

Viadero, D. (2007, August 1). Study: Low, high fliers gain less under NCLB. *Education Week,* 7.

Vohr, B. (2003). Infants and children with hearing loss—Part 2: Overview. *Mental Retardation and Developmental Disabilities Research Reviews, 9,* 218–219.

Wall, S., Davis, K., Crowley, A., & White, L. (2005). The urban paraeducator goes to college. *Remedial and Special Education, 26,* 183–190.

Walsh, K. (2004). Through the looking glass: How NCLB's promise requires facing hard truths about teacher quality. *The Clearing House, 78,* 22–25. Heldref Publications.

Wang, Y., Trezek, B., Luckner, J., & Paul, P. (2008). The role of phonology and phonologically related skills in reading instruction for students who are deaf or hard of hearing. *American Annals of the Deaf, 153,* 396–407.

Webb-Johnson, G., Artiles, A., Trent, S., Jackson, C., & Velox, A. (1998). The status of research on multicultural education in teacher education and special education. *Remedial and Special Education, 19,* 7–15.

Weiner, D. (2006). *Alternate assessments measured against grade-level achievement standards: The Massachusetts "Competency Portfolio"* (Synthesis Report No. 59). Minneapolis: University of Minnesota, National Center on Educational Outcomes. Retrieved from http://www.cehd.umn.edu/NCEO/OnlinePubs/Synthesis59.html.

Wilbur, R. (2000). The use of ASL to support the development of English and literacy. *Journal of Deaf Studies and Deaf Education, 5,* 81–104.

Wiley, H. I., Thurlow, M. L., & Klein, J. A. (2005). *Steady progress: State public reporting practices for students with disabilities after the first year of NCLB (2002–2003)* (Technical Report No. 40). Minneapolis, MN: University of Minnesota, National Center on Educational Outcomes. Retrieved from http://education.umn.edu/NCEO/OnlinePubs/Technical40.htm.

Wilmshurst, L., & Brue, A. (2005). Parents guide to special education: Insider advice on how to navigate the system and help your child succeed. Washington, DC: American Management Association.

Wright, P. W., & Wright, P. D. (2005). *Your child's IEP: Practical and legal guidance for parents.* Retrieved from http://www.wrightslaw.com/advoc/articles/iep_guidance.html.

Wright, P. W., Wright, P. D., & Heath, S. W. (2003). *Wrightslaw: No Child Left Behind.* Hartfield, VA: Harbor House Law Press.

Yoshinaga-Itano, C., & Gravel, J. (2001). The evidence for universal newborn hearing screening. *American Journal of Audiology, 10,* 62–64. doi:10.1044/1059-0889(2001/013).

Zaitseva, G., Pursglove, M., & Gregory, S. (1999). Vygotsky, sign language, and the education of deaf pupils. *Journal of Deaf Studies and Deaf Education, 4,* 9–16.

Zeichner, K. (1999). The new scholarship in teacher education. *Educational Researcher, 28*(9), 4–15.

Zinkil, S., & Gilbert, T. (2000). Parents' view: What to consider when contemplating inclusion. *Intervention in School and Clinic, 35,* 224–227.

Index

Figures and tables are indicated with f and t following the page number.